2-0877
2006

Moving On

Moving On

Dump Your Relationship Baggage and Make Room for the Love of Your Life

Russell Friedman and John W. James

M. Evans

Lanham • New York • Boulder • Toronto • Plymouth, UK

Published by M. Evans
An imprint of The Rowman & Littlefield Publishing Group, Inc.
4501 Forbes Boulevard, Suite 200, Lanham, Maryland 20706

Estover Road
Plymouth PL6 7PY
United Kingdom

Distributed by NATIONAL BOOK NETWORK

Library of Congress Cataloging-in-Publication Data Available

ISBN-13: 978-1-59077-127-3
ISBN-10: 1-59077-127-3

∞™ The paper used in this publication meets the minimum
requirements of American National Standard for Information
Sciences—Permanence of Paper for Printed Library Materials,
ANSI/NISO Z39.48–1992.
Manufactured in the United States of America.

CONTENTS

ACKNOWLEDGMENTS

We would have to go into the phone book of every city in the United States to find all the people we need to acknowledge. Then we'd have to do the same in Europe, the Middle East, and Asia to find the many others who have opened their hearts to let us help them. We want to thank all of those courageous souls. They were able to show up at our workshops and trainings and trust us to guide them.

There are some individuals we need to thank for their contributions. First and foremost, we thank our agent and friend, Jennifer Unter. We also thank P. J. Dempsey and Matt Harper for getting this project off the ground.

We thank Eric Cline, our partner and friend in Canada. And we thank Anders Magnusson, our partner and friend in Sweden.

Over the years, we've added others who expand our ability to help as many broken hearts as possible. We want to acknowledge each of them individually: Steve Moeller, Nancy Stutz-Martin, Debi Frankle, Elaine Henderson, and Lois Hall.

As with most organizations, there's usually one central person who makes the whole thing work. For us, that person is Lisa Laughlin, who single-handedly keeps us in the pink. North Carolina gave us one of its finest exports, Rhoda Cerny, who helps us help the broken hearts that call here for guidance every day. We also want to acknowledge Esther Walker, who walked us through some of the trying times as we worked to make this book as good as it can be.

Thank you.
Russell and John
Sherman Oaks, California

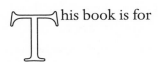

INTRODUCTION

This book is for

- anyone who has experienced the end of a romantic relationship, whether recent or long ago;
- anyone who has experienced a string of broken romances and is tired of the merry-go-round;
- anyone who recognizes that their current romantic involvement is on rocky ground but doesn't know why or what to do about it;
- anyone who has stopped trying to find happiness in a romantic relationship, believing that it just isn't possible.

The Quest for a Soul Mate

"Am I ever going to find the man or woman of my dreams?"

That's one question, here's another: "Why do I always sabotage my relationships?" How about this comment? "No matter how hard I try, I can't seem to get it right." Or "All my relationships eventually die a horrible death." Or "Why do I always pick the wrong people?" Does any of this sound familiar? We'd guess that you hear those things a lot—or you find yourself saying them.

We hear them all, because we talk with people every day who are grieving the end of a romantic relationship. We've been doing that for nearly three decades. Underneath those questions and comments, what we hear most often is the desire to find a "soul mate." The quest begins in early childhood and continues throughout life despite most people experiencing so many unsuccessful relationships.

Current statistics report a divorce rate near 50 percent. But that number is a pittance compared to the romantic relationships that end before there is a marriage. When there has been no marriage, there are no statistics to show just how large the problem is. Based on our informal surveys, the ratio may be as high as forty failed relationships for each formal divorce. Statistics aside, there can be no doubt that the string of unresolved relationships people drag with them limits the potential for success in future relationships.

Excess Emotional Baggage

Excess baggage typically refers to luggage that exceeds the allowance you can check for free when you travel by air. The obvious reason for the limitation is to keep the weight of the aircraft less than a certain amount. If an airplane is overloaded, it may have difficulty getting off the ground. Even if it does take off, it may have trouble maintaining level flight. If we correlate those ideas to romantic relationships, we could use the phrase **excess emotional baggage** and draw the same conclusions. Emotional baggage is what people often carry into relationships. A relationship in which one or both of the partners is overloaded with baggage from prior relationships will have problems. If it manages to get safely off the ground, it still may have trouble maintaining level, loving flight. When those relationships crash, people will say that one or both of the participants was carrying excess emotional baggage.

About Us

At first you might be surprised to find that we are the founders of The Grief Recovery Institute®. If you're like most people, you associate the word grief exclusively with death. But in reality, a romantic breakup is the "death" of a relationship. It ends the hopes, dreams, and expectations that we have about the future. The fact remains that we feel grief following the change or end of any familiar pattern of behavior.

The Grief Recovery Institute was founded on a simple premise—to deliver assistance to the largest number of people in the shortest period of time. In our previous books we addressed the two largest problems that exist in the world as they relate to grief. *The Grief Recovery Handbook*, first published in 1986, focused primarily on the grief caused by death. For most people, seeing the words "grief recovery" together marked their first awareness that recovery from painful emotional losses was even possible. Next, we took direct aim at the huge number of parents, grandparents, and other guardians who were desperate to learn better ways to guide their children in dealing with the losses that affect their young lives. *When Children Grieve*, published in 2001, addressed the entire gamut of losses that are most likely to impact children. It gives adults concrete tools and actions to guide the children in their care.

The Grief Recovery Handbook and *When Children Grieve* each developed and refined a system to complete what is left emotionally unfinished by a death, a divorce, or other major losses. At latest count, the books have been translated into seven languages, and more are on the way. Using the books as the basic text, we have instituted several thousand Grief Recovery Outreach Programs and Helping Children Deal with Loss Programs throughout the world. The groups are facilitated by the certified Grief ❣ Recovery® Specialists we have trained. They have adopted our mutual goal of providing effective assistance to as many grieving people as quickly as possible. They have also been in the forefront of developing and perfecting the program in this book, which is designed to help people complete the emotional damage of their romantic past.

It's one thing to tell you what we've done to help others, but it's another to explain that in order to help others we first had to help ourselves. Not only is that true for us but we believe it should be the cornerstone for all who would guide others. We are both in very happy, long-term marital relationships, one of twenty-five years, the other eighteen, but that is only part of what qualifies us to write this book. Both of us also had failed relationships, which is just another piece of what qualifies us to write this book. What uniquely qualifies us is that we have taken the actions outlined in this book to complete the prior romantic relationships that affected our lives. It is the emotional completion that resulted from those actions that allowed us each to find and sustain our long-term relationships. In turn, that's what qualifies and encourages us to help others

The Expanding Challenge of Relationships

It's almost impossible to go through a day without hearing yet another story of a couple who broke up. And we're talking about what we hear in our social lives not just at the Grief Recovery Institute. With that in mind, it was time for us to set out a plan of action, in book form, that would help an unlimited number of people learn how to effectively complete past romantic relationships. After doing that, they could move forward and avoid the pitfalls that had been keeping them from success in relationships. What's the problem? Why can't people achieve their dreams? Even though people have the willingness to try to find true love, they keep failing to get over the hurdles that keep them from achieving their goals.

Years ago, we began making extensive notes on the problem of breakup or divorce, since it was such a constant issue presented by the people who came to our seminars and trainings. Tangled among their other losses were the inevitable stories of failed romantic relationships. Using the same basic ideas that helped people complete other kinds of relationships, we developed a program that could be applied directly to romantic relationships. We road tested the evolving program with our seminar attendees, who were more than eager to have real actions to help them deal effectively with past relationships. Those courageous people worked hard to end the cycle of sadness that their failed relationships had brought. By completing the past painful events, they were able to acquire better tools for ensuring success in their next romantic relationship. We are grateful to them for providing the proof positive of the life-affirming actions in this book.

In our seminars we discovered that those who wanted to find happiness in relationships didn't lack willingness or courage. What they lacked was correct information and a safe environment in which to take the new actions we showed them. Simply put, since people don't know how to grieve and complete relationships that end, they carry the unresolved emotions forward into future relationships. This almost guarantees the next ending. With no tools for completing the end of relationship number one, they simply use the same wrong tools when the second relationship ends. What is incomplete from each prior relationship accumulates and is then dragged into successive relationships. It becomes the emotional baggage that is referred to when relationships have ended.

Sadness Is Not Gender Specific

There is much written about the role that gender plays in relationships, but not by us. As you read this book, you'll notice there is very little mention of gender. In part I, when we talk about the ideas we all learned for dealing with the painful emotions caused by relationship endings, it will become clear to you that sadness is not exclusive to either gender. A broken heart is a broken heart is a broken heart.

Understanding Completion

If you suspect that you're carrying emotional baggage, then it makes sense to say that you haven't completed what was unfinished. While the idea of becoming emotionally complete makes sense, most people don't know what to do to achieve it. That's what this book is for. Completion is the result of a series of actions that help you discover and communicate what was left emotionally unfinished at the time a relationship ended.

It is the shift from intellect to emotions that helps people discover and complete what is left unfinished when a relationship ends.

As the book unfolds, you'll learn what those actions are and how to do them. As a consequence of those actions, you'll achieve emotional completion with prior relationships. You'll then have the freedom to participate fully in a romantic relationship. An added bonus of completion is the ability to listen to and follow your intuition. This will enhance your ability to choose the person with whom you can develop a long-lasting relationship.

All Relationships Are Unique

The more we worked with people dealing with relationship endings, the more obvious it became that the key to recovery lay in the simple idea that all relationships are unique. There are no exceptions to that rule. One person's relationship with a dad who had died might be radically different from the relationship a brother or sister had with that same parent. One relationship might have been glorious and the other horrific, each of which would produce different emotional reactions. When dealing with romantic endings it's equally apparent that the key to recovery resides within the uniqueness of each individual relationship and the end of the unrealized hopes and dreams about the future.

People are often encouraged to believe that there is a bond with others who had a comparable loss. Although it may sound right, it doesn't really make sense. It's the unfortunate by-product of the emergence of overly specific support groups that tend to segregate grievers based on the loss they experienced. The problem is that it presumes that everyone in the group had the same kind of relationship with the person who died or with whom they had a romantic relationship. Nothing could be further from the truth.

While romantic relationships are different than other personal bonds, they still leave behind unfinished emotional communications when they end. We discovered that the same tools that helped someone complete what was left emotionally unfinished when a loved one died apply to completing romantic relationships that did not make it all the way to "till death do us part."

Better Knowledge, Better Results

"Will this book give me better knowledge and new actions so I can complete prior relationships and not sabotage future ones?" Absolutely! We know that sounds like a bold promise, so let us explain why we're so confident. We'd guess you've read other books. They may have helped you understand what happened and even why, but they didn't teach you how to complete your prior relationships so you could to do things differently and get better results. This book contains a series of actions that will provide real solutions for you. The actions that will help you complete past relationships are the difference between this book and many others. The same applies to other methods of self-examination, whether or not they involve the use of a book.

To get to the solution, however, you will need to do some in-depth and often difficult work. There's no easy way. We'll guide you every step of the way. Endings are often inevitable and always painful, but with the right information there's no reason to drag old relationships into new ones.

We wish you good luck.

Russell and John

PS: If you find yourself throwing this book across the room or yelling at us once in a while, we will understand.

PART I

Identifying the Problem

The idea that people carry emotional baggage from prior relationships into new ones is more than just a figure of speech. It's a reality. Since most people do it, it's likely that you have also. As you become more able to see that about yourself, you may realize that you have sabotaged relationships or chosen to be in relationships that never had a chance.

To see what you've done and how you've done it, it's essential that you identify the basic ideas you acquired for dealing with the emotions connected to losses of every kind. It's important to acquire this awareness so you can identify and dump the emotional baggage that you have dragged with you.

How to Use This Book

It would sound authoritarian for us to say, "Read every word and do every exercise as stated." So we'll use the softer approach and *suggest* that you read every word and do every exercise as stated. The actions laid out in this book have worked for thousands of people. If you're willing, they'll work for you as well. The key is taking the actions. Just reading what is contained here isn't enough. Caution: if you look for exceptions, you'll find them, magnify them, and rationalize continuing along the path you're on. That would not give you the new results you want.

"**You cannot think your way into right action but you can act your way into right thinking**." We don't know who first said that, but it makes it profoundly clear that action is the key to helping us accomplish meaningful changes in our lives. As it relates to this book, we can paraphrase it to say, "You cannot read your way into a successful relationship, but you can read and *then take the actions* that will lead you to a successful one." The actions will be in the form of a series of exercises that begin in chapter 2.

If you're ready, let's get to work.

CHAPTER

ONE

EVERYONE HAS EMOTIONAL BAGGAGE, EVEN YOU

At almost every social gathering, you will hear conversations about somebody's breakup or divorce. The question is always asked, "Did he have a lot of baggage?" Without exception the answer is yes. What usually follows is an attempt to commiserate with the aggrieved party: "Don't feel bad, you'll do better next time" and other such clichés. The attempt to soothe is always well intentioned but rarely helpful.

While the question about the other person's baggage may be reasonable, the blind spot exists in the absence of the more important question that is hardly ever asked. **And how much baggage did *you* bring to the relationship?** Admittedly, it sounds like a cruel question. Yet it is the only question that can force anyone to identify and jettison their own excess cargo before attempting to take flight in a long-term committed relationship.

Most of us understand what is meant when the word *baggage* is used in the context of a failed relationship. When we expand it and call it emotional baggage, it becomes a little clearer. Now we need to define it even more so we can get you into the actions that will lead you from the problem to the solution.

Emotional baggage is many things:

- the general misinformation we have all learned about how to deal with loss
- the specific misinformation we acquire about our emotional reactions to romantic relationships that have ended
- the short-term habits we develop in reaction to romantic endings, which become long-term and get dragged into future relationships
- the accumulation of undelivered emotional communications we store after romantic relationships end

Since you can't deal with anybody's baggage but your own, we're going to start with you and yours.

What You Learn Is What You Do

We start learning about the painful feelings of loss very early in life, as soon as things are taken away from us. It does not feel good when the things we have become attached to, like stuffed animal toys or baby blankets, get taken away. While that might seem like an illogical starting point for a book about romantic relationships, it is nonetheless exactly where we must begin. These early losses, and the guidance of the people around us, dictate how we react later when our first romantic relationship ends.

Emotional Baggage Is Acquired

Velveteen Rabbit

Assume for a moment that when you were born you carried no baggage of any kind. You were not carrying any incorrect information or any incomplete relationships into the new adventure of life. You could react to life as it occurred, in the moment. If something delighted you, you laughed. Once that feeling ended you were ready to participate in the next emotional experience that came along. Let's say that the next experience was a sad one. No problem, you cried. Again, in a short time, the crying was done. You stored nothing and were ready to take on life's next event.

In either case, happy or sad, you notified the world around you as to exactly how you felt. It was a perfect system. Think about it. If no feelings were stored, then no emotional baggage was created. It's likely that for the first few years of your life you processed all emotions naturally, in the moment you had them. But as you moved from infancy to toddlerhood, you began to learn that communicating all of your feelings, happy or sad, was no longer accepted and rewarded. You were being told and shown that some feelings were not okay. The ones that were off limits were sad or negative. The display of tears that often accompanies those feelings was equally not supported. Most people remember a line like this from their childhood: "If you're going to cry, go to your room." We doubt that you ever heard, "If you're going to be happy, go to your room."

The idea that happy feelings are okay and sad ones are not puts children in conflict with their own natural reactions to life events. It is that overriding idea that makes it difficult for us to deal with the emotions we feel when something sad happens. We are going to help you look at all the information that you learned about how to deal with your emotions to see which must be discarded. Then you can realign yourself with what is emotionally truthful for you. Don't worry, we aren't going to encourage you to revert to acting like a two-year-old. There are honest and open ways to communicate how you feel without becoming infantile. We are confident that as you begin to recognize the general ideas we mention, you will find within them the specific ideas that have kept you stuck.

How Our Minds Store Information

The human mind is the ultimate hard drive. It is the most sophisticated storage device that exists. From the moment we draw our first breath, our mind engages. It observes everything we see, taste, touch, hear, or smell. It misses nothing. It forgets nothing. Many people find this hard to believe, yet it is true. Here's an example: Almost everybody's childhood memories include comments like, "Clean up your plate, children are starving in [name a country]." This powerful message usually came from our parents. We took the idea that we had to eat everything on our plates as a piece of absolute truth because our parents said it was so. As we got older, some of us learned to modify that message and found our own healthy eating habits. Sadly, many have not.

Here's another example: Do you remember a smell that you associate with your grandmother's house? Maybe the smell of a cedar-lined closet jumps to mind. The memory was embedded when you were very young and has been carried forward for a long time. It's still there now, though you may not have thought about it consciously for many years. Even so, you probably had no trouble finding it. How many years has it been there? Just remember that your mind never forgets. All it took was the stimulus of a question for you to search for and remember that smell.

How We Learn

Experts suggest that by the age of three 75 percent of the basic information that we will use to run our lives has been observed, coded, and recorded. The information is stored with an attached intensity based on the source of the information. The most powerful early influences are usually mom and dad and other immediate family members. The same experts indicate that during the next ten to twelve years teachers, classmates, movies, television programs, song lyrics, magazine articles, and other sources contribute another 20 percent to the ideas that we learn and use. By the time we reach adolescence and our first romantic relationship, 95 percent of the basic information we will use to interpret and operate our lives is already in place.

Conscious memory starts at the point in time when we can first remember things as we look back over our lives. Memory experts have found that the dawn of conscious memory happens somewhere between the ages of three and six, usually closer to six. That means that those things that happened before the onset of conscious memory are not directly accessible. That is why no matter how hard we try, we can't always figure out why we believe certain things and why we feel the way we do.

We Assume that What We Know Is Right

Our young minds perceive all incoming information as always right. We absorb everything that comes in through our senses without any prior information for comparison. When we are very young, we do not have any way to distinguish good information from bad. There is no filter to help us evaluate the information we are absorbing. However, as we said earlier, since the information has come from influential sources, we give it the value of absolute rightness and it becomes etched into our memories.

A unique piece of language is used to describe the accumulation of information we use to run our lives. In abbreviated form we call it BS, which is short for belief system, and everyone's got one. Your belief system is made up of all the information that has ever been stored in your brain. Everything that you believe, you believe to be right. The vast majority of information stored in your personal hard drive is correct, helpful, and life affirming.

But some of what we learn when we're young isn't helpful at all. This is especially true in the area of dealing with sad feelings. Since sad or painful feelings are the normal and natural reaction to relationship endings, what we learned in childhood about dealing with those feelings is of crucial importance. If we learned incorrect ideas about dealing with sadness, we will still have invested them with the same "rightness." In addition, we will have practiced using them for many years before our first romantic breakup and will use them again out of habit.

Let's apply the metaphor of excess baggage to the idea of the rightness of our belief systems. The incorrect information in our belief system becomes part of the baggage we carry forward. We defend everything we do from a position of rightness even if it causes us to make the same mistakes time after time. Clearly this is not a good path to follow.

CHAPTER TWO

SIX MYTHS ABOUT SADNESS

ix major myths limit our ability to deal with sad feelings. Those myths contain the incorrect information that most of us use when a relationship ends. That stored information is part of your belief system, which you consider to be right. As we help you uncover what you were taught about dealing with sadness, you'll realize that much of what you learned might be called *intellectual baggage*. You'll become aware that you have never taken a close look at your beliefs about sadness to see if they are accurate and helpful for you. The repetitive use of unhelpful ideas is what creates the emotional baggage that has limited your ability to participate openly and fully in your relationships.

Ideally, the mind, the emotions, and the intuition work in harmony. This allows us to deal effectively with all the major events in our lives. Most young children participate in life with all three of these aspects connected and functioning. Since young children can process feelings in the moment they happen, no feelings are being stored. One of the reasons that young children can be so magnificent is that they can move easily between intellect, emotions, and intuition. The expression of emotions, along with the use of the intellect and intuition, helps keep children (and adults) in harmony with their nature. When the emotional component is limited, we lose our natural ability to deal with sad feelings.

Myth 1: Don't Feel Bad

A child's early life is fine until the day he or she first hears three very unfortunate words—**Don't feel bad!** Those three words have lifelong negative impact. At first glance they may not seem dangerous, but closer inspection reveals a serious problem. Up until the moment a child hears and understands those words, all of his or her feelings were accepted and allowed. Then something shifts, and from that point forward, only joy and laughter are encouraged. Sadness and tears are no longer part of the equation.

The classic example of this shift happens when a little girl returns from preschool with tears in her eyes.

When asked what happened, she replies, "The other little girls were mean to me." The parent says, "Don't feel bad. Here, have a cookie; you'll feel better." When we look closely, we see that the message has two parts. First, it tells the child not to feel what she is already feeling. Second, it tells her to use a substance to distract her from feeling bad. There are major unhelpful consequences to the idea contained in the simple phrase "don't feel bad."

Equally common is for a child to come home upset and, when asked what happened, say, "The other children were mean to me." To which the parent replies, "Don't feel bad. You'll make new friends." Keep this in mind, because in just a moment you're going to see how the second half of that statement contains another myth.

Because the messages advising the child not to feel bad come from an adult authority source, they have the stamp of rightness on them. They are logged into the little girl's belief system as right. Until that point she has trusted her parents and told them everything, truthfully. When asked the question, "What happened?" she naturally believed that she could trust her parents with her feelings. Now she discovers she was wrong. This represents a 180-degree shift from when she was younger and all of her feelings were okay. Now her sad feelings have not only become unacceptable but they must be bypassed by covering them up with food or, in the second example, by making new friends. It puts the child in conflict with her own natural emotions, those of feeling hurt by what happened with the other children. It also puts her in conflict with her natural desire to tell someone she trusts about how she feels. This phenomenon is not limited to little girls. Exactly the same conversation happens with little boys. "Don't feel bad" is administered equally to both genders.

Myth 2: Replace the Loss

You might think that more life-affecting events than hurt feelings at the playground would be dealt with differently, but you would be wrong. When John was seven years old, his dog Peggy died. Peggy was his constant companion and best friend. John was overwhelmed with emotion when she died. Seeing his pain his dad said, "Don't feel bad, on Saturday we'll get you a new dog." The second part of that phrase translates into **replace the loss**. John's heart was broken, and the idea of getting a new dog added an illogical element to an already painful and confusing event. The message John received had two parts:

> **Don't feel bad.**
> **Replace the loss.**

John's parents kept their word and got John a new dog on Saturday. But John was still reeling from the impact of Peggy's death and he was unable to connect with the new dog. Looking back, he realizes that his heart was broken. He just couldn't allow himself to attach to another dog. He couldn't risk getting hurt again, so he gave the new dog to his younger brother.

As we see the idea of "replace the loss" when John's dog died, we can also reflect on the comment the little girl heard when the other children didn't want to be her friends. "Don't feel bad, you can make new friends," gives a clear message that she should somehow replace the friends. This establishes a belief that will be a real problem for her years later when she experiences her first romantic breakup.

And Then Came the Fish

When Russell was in the eighth grade, he fell in love with a girl named Karen. They talked about everything. They told each other their most important truths and secrets. They made plans for their future together. He trusted her more than he'd ever trusted anyone before. Life was good. Then one day Karen decided that she didn't want to be Russell's girlfriend anymore. He was crushed. He remembers the dark days and weeks that followed. He couldn't eat, he couldn't sleep, and he didn't want to see or talk to anybody. After several days, his mom, trying to console him, said, "**Don't feel bad, there are plenty of fish in the sea.**"

That was the first time Russell knew that he had been dating a fish. Sorry, we couldn't resist a little joke here, but almost everybody has heard some version of that line after a breakup. Humor aside, the message Russell got from an important authority source—his own mother—was that he shouldn't feel bad and he should go right out and get another girlfriend. So he did. But he was not eager to tell the new girlfriend everything and get hurt again, so he held back. He did not feel that he could trust her. After all, his last girlfriend had broken his trust, so he certainly wasn't going to expose himself to that kind of hurt again. Not if he could help it. Little did he realize that by holding back, he was going to ruin that relationship. When it ended a short time later, she said, "I don't want to be with you because you never let me know who you really are." By age fourteen, Russell had already tried to limit the pain of the first breakup by rushing into a new relationship. Not only did it fail to reduce the emotional pain but it also made him more fearful, and he withheld even more the next time. Without realizing it, Russell was beginning to accumulate the emotional baggage that he would drag into future relationships.

There is an interesting similarity in the three different scenarios. After the first breakup, Russell had been instructed, just like the little girl from the preschool and like John after his dog died, with exactly the same ideas:

Don't feel bad.
Replace the loss.

When we hear those messages they become the default settings we will use when similar events happen later in our lives. When romantic relationships end, we will automatically believe that we shouldn't feel bad and we should go right out and find another love. Why? Because those messages have been pounded into us since we were in preschool. Trying not to feel bad when we do inevitably compounds the problem, since it doesn't allow us to be honest with ourselves. Activating replace the loss by jumping into a new relationship when we are still raw from the end of the previous one makes no sense and almost guarantees failure.

Replace the loss doesn't work for a few simple and obvious reasons: **All relationships are unique; there are no exceptions.** And **relationships are neither replaceable nor interchangeable.**

Myth 3: Grieve Alone

"Laugh and the whole world laughs with you; cry, and you cry alone," is a powerful message that can have life-long negative impact. You've already been told not to feel bad, but when you do you are told to isolate yourself from others. During your childhood, you probably also heard the classic "If you're going to cry, go to your room." You may have heard comments like that when you had normal emotional reactions to sad events and tried to share them with the people you trusted. By the time a child is fifteen years old, he or she will have received more than twenty-three thousand messages that sad or painful feelings should not be communicated to others. The comments that contribute to the idea that we should grieve alone also suggest that we should leave others alone to deal with their sad feelings. "She needs her space" is often said as the natural by-product of the incorrect idea that sad feelings should not be shared with others. It leads to further isolation at precisely the time that she might really need to talk about her feelings.

In addition, we observed what happened when others showed sad or painful feelings. We heard comments like "She lost it" or "He broke down." Those remarks reinforced the idea that it was not safe to communicate sad feelings in front of others. It doesn't take many of those observations to break our sense of safety and convince us to isolate ourselves. The idea that we must keep sad feelings to ourselves becomes another "always right" message in our belief systems. As a result, when we feel sad, our mental computers send us an instant message telling us not to burden others with our feelings. Our response to that message is to isolate ourselves and hold back our feelings.

Conflicting Feelings

The mixture of feelings we have when a relationship ends might seem to conflict with each other. On one hand, we may feel relieved that the arguing is over, and on the other, we may be heartbroken that the dreams for the future have ended. Relief usually feels positive, and heartbreak feels negative. It is normal to want to communicate all the feelings we have when a relationship ends. That's where another conflict occurs. While we want to tell others how we feel, the constantly reinforced message to grieve alone confuses us.

There's a broad range of emotions we're liable to experience as part of the grief following a romantic breakup. Feeling sad in reaction to a painful event is normal, as is communicating those feelings to the people we trust. The problem is that we've been taught that we aren't supposed to feel them—"don't feel bad"—and if you do, you should feel them in private—"if you're going to cry, go to your room." The bottom-line message at a time when we might most need and want the support and love of others is **grieve alone**.

Grieving alone is the third major incorrect idea that impedes our ability to complete the emotions brought on by romantic endings. Our list has grown a little longer:

Don't feel bad.
Replace the loss.
Grieve alone.

All in all, a sure-fire recipe for the accumulation of emotional baggage and future relationship disasters.

Myth 4: Time Heals All Wounds

Of all the incorrect ideas related to dealing with romantic breakups, this one is probably the most life limiting of all. It is stated in many different ways, but each variation is equally wrong. The most common phrases are **"time heals all wounds"** or **"it just takes time."** We've never met anyone who was not brainwashed with that totally false idea.

The best way to explain why this idea is so wrong is to use the analogy of a flat tire. Imagine that you go out to your car and notice that it has a flat tire. Would you pull up a chair, sit down, and wait for air to jump back into the tire? We didn't think so. Imagine someone sitting in front of a flat tire waiting for time to fix it. It's a funny picture, isn't it? We all know that to get that car back on the road, an action will have to be taken. Most of us would call the auto club and ask them to send out someone to change the flat for us (that's one of the main reasons we have cell phones, right?). Some of us would actually get out the jack and do it ourselves. Either way, an action has to happen before the car can be driven safely.

Here's the emotional parallel. A broken heart is an awful lot like a flat tire. The get-up-and-go has got up and gone. It's very difficult to participate fully in life when your heart is broken. **Waiting for time to heal your heart without taking any actions is as foolish as waiting for air to jump back into a flat tire.**

We can take that analogy one step further: imagine that instead of repairing the flat tire, you just get in the car and start driving. That assumes that you could actually drive the car in a straight line and survive. Pretty soon you will not only have destroyed the tire but you will be riding on the rim, which will destroy the wheel. Now transfer that to the relationship world. You drive your heart into a new relationship even though you have done nothing to discover and complete what was left emotionally unfinished by the ending of the last one. Let's face it, while you're trying to deal with the aftermath of your prior relationship, you're not really available for a new one. Think of it as riding around on the rim of your heart, putting inordinate pressure on it while it's still flattened. Now you're driving and parking your broken heart in someone else's driveway. Not a very nice picture, is it?

Linking Bad Ideas Doesn't Help

Putting two bad ideas together just makes a bigger mess. Starting to date when you haven't yet dealt with the just-ended relationship is what we've already identified as "replace the loss." It carries with it the likelihood of sabotaging the new relationship. Equally dangerous are any suggestions that time is the primary component that indicates when you can start dating again. **All time-based ideas about being ready to date are false**. We've heard one that says that it takes half the amount of time that you were in the relationship for you to be ready for a new one. That means that if you were married for ten years, you'd have to wait five years before you could begin to date. It's a bad plan for a lot of reasons, but the worst one may be the implication that all you have to do is wait for time to pass. What are you supposed to do with your life in the meantime?

Some suggestions are more poetic than others: "You must go through four seasons, and then you'll be ready." It sounds wonderful, even romantic in an odd way. But the truth is you could go through a thousand seasons if you are emotionally incomplete and never feel safe to love and trust again. The underlying message that **time heals all wounds** is false.

Our list has grown to the following:

Don't feel bad.
Replace the loss.
Grieve alone.
Time heals all wounds.

Myth 5: Be Strong

Another incorrect idea we were taught is that we have to **be strong** when dealing with the emotions connected to loss. Being strong further disconnects us from our normal and healthy response to sad events. Being strong implies that we should not demonstrate our sad feelings to others. If you think about the phrase *be strong* in the context of emotions, it suggests that having and displaying sad feelings would indicate that you are weak.

Over time, being strong has gotten tangled up with the idea that only little children can express sadness, because being grown-up means that you don't show those feelings. Many people are familiar with the famous song, "Big Girls Don't Cry." It was the number one song in America for five weeks in 1962. It may seem like ancient history, but the song title stands out as yet another indicator that we must be strong. It also implies that if you show sad feelings, you might be a burden on others, as if your sadness was an infectious disease.

The idea of being strong for ourselves implies that we also have to **be strong for others**. Frankly, we can't understand how that could possibly be helpful to someone else. If I lie and hide my feelings, how can it help you feel safe enough to communicate your sad feelings? It's actually backward. When I portray myself as having no sad feelings, it suggests that you shouldn't either.

We'd guess that you've never looked at the idea of being strong in quite this way before. Based on our thirty years of helping people, we believe that being emotionally honest is what being strong really looks like. That means telling the truth about how you feel, and if there are some emotions attached to that truth, so be it. In the end, we give people a simple choice: **be strong or be human, pick one.**

Our expanding list now includes the following:

Don't feel bad.
Replace the loss.
Grieve alone.
Time heals all wounds.
Be strong.

Myth 6: Keep Busy

Keep busy is the most common piece of bad advice doled out to broken-hearted people. It's another dangerous idea that you need to recognize. We've seen people turn into human cyclones trying to follow that counsel. We've seen them exhaust themselves and worse. "Keep busy" is really an extension of "time heals all wounds." The hidden idea is that if you can just stay busy and distract yourself from what you're feeling, then another day will go by and time will heal you. Absurd, isn't it?

There's nothing intrinsically wrong with being busy, but it's not logical advice for dealing with your emotions. As most of you will realize, it's very hard to concentrate in the days and weeks following a breakup. That alone makes it difficult to stay focused on any task and also puts you in danger of making errors or having lapses in judgment. You'll also recognize that the feelings that follow the end of a relationship are mentally exhausting and physically draining. Substituting busyness for more effective ways of dealing with those emotions can cause major problems in many other life areas.

Many people use work as a way of keeping busy, believing that they're being more productive. Still others will clean obsessively or rearrange furniture. But no matter what form it takes, keeping busy is a distraction from the feelings connected to the end of the relationship. Worse, it acts to bury them, and they can come back and haunt you later. It's reasonable to presume that any feelings that we keep bottled up inside are not really gone, they're just hidden. Keeping busy merely creates an illusion of well-being, caught in the swirl of activity we use to distract ourselves. It's also reasonable to presume that there may be negative emotional or physical consequences when we do not communicate our feelings. As you can imagine, keeping busy is a far cry from the infant who was allowed and encouraged to express all feelings in the moment he had them.

Exercise 1: Identifying the Myths You've Used

Now it's your turn to participate in the first of a series of exercises that will help you discard the baggage that has been limiting you. All you need is a pen and a notebook that you will use and then put safely away after each exercise.

This exercise is simple. Write down the list of six myths we've just outlined and think about whether you learned any or all of them. They represent the most common incorrect ideas that you may have been influenced to believe about dealing with sad, painful, or negative emotions.

Don't feel bad.
Replace the loss.
Grieve alone.
Time heals all wounds.
Be strong.
Keep busy.

Circle the ones you most relate to and then think about which ones you've used most often since your last relationship ended. As you do this, you might think of other things you learned about dealing with sad feelings. If you think of any, write them down. With your new awareness, you may realize that they weren't really helpful. After you make your notes put your notebook in a safe and private place.

CHAPTER THREE

FEELINGS— GOOD, BAD, AND UGLY

Feelings come in all shapes and sizes: good, bad, and sometimes ugly. We all have feelings, and we express them in our own unique ways. Some of us are very vocal about them, some of us are more private. But one thing we could probably agree on is that the buildup of feelings has negative consequences in our lives. More specifically, when we hold onto feelings, we limit our ability to find and participate fully in a relationship. To learn how to deal more effectively with our feelings, we need to have a better understanding of what feelings really are.

What Is a Feeling?

A great deal of this book is about how we deal with the feelings connected to relationship endings. With that in mind, we think it's important for you to understand what we mean when we talk about feelings. **A feeling is a physical reaction to a thought**. That's our definition, and it's parallel to what you'd find in the dictionary. We also need to establish that the definition applies to all feelings, whether they are in reaction to positive or negative thoughts. For our purposes, *feelings* and *emotions* are interchangeable words.

Here's how we apply our definition. When we get bad news we might report that it feels like a punch in the stomach. In reaction to sad news we may feel choked up or even struggle with our breathing. These are very physical reactions to the information we have just received. The same is true when we get good news. The exhilaration we feel in our bodies when we learn of something positive is expressed in many physical ways. To *jump for joy* is just one example of a physical reaction to good news. It's very helpful to have a sense of physical reaction when talking about our feelings, in part because it makes the communication very clear. That's important because at the very least we hope that we'll be heard and understood. The more accurately we report our feelings, the more likely we'll feel as if others understand what we're saying.

Russell recalls what it felt like when his first wife told him that she was leaving him. "It was all in my chest, like I'd been hit by a truck. That was followed by an emptiness, as if my heart had been torn out of my body." Reading that description, you can immediately understand what Russell felt when he heard the news. It's not open to interpretation or analysis. It's a clear example of a **feeling being a physical reaction to a thought**. One of the reasons it's so understandable is that nearly everyone has experienced some kind of event that produced that kind of bodily response. But even if they haven't, the idea that something feels like a hit in the chest is not vague, it is concrete and understandable. It doesn't tell any of the thoughts or ideas that ran through Russell's brain, just the feelings.

Russell's wife told him she was leaving over the phone. Until then, he had no inkling that his wife was so terribly unhappy in the marriage. At best, he knew that they'd had their struggles as a couple but nothing that he thought serious enough to end the marriage. For Russell it was like a sudden death. But an unexpected ending like that is not the only kind that produces strong feelings.

We know that people are often affected by *how* the relationship ended. We know that they can be affected by *who* ended the relationship. We know there is impact *when* the ending comes as the result of problems that built up over a long time. And we know that people sometimes feel ambushed *when* there's been a sudden, unexpected ending, as in Russell's case. In addition to the emotions experienced as they relate to the how, who, and when, the ending itself creates feelings. Even those who wanted a relationship to end for a long time report powerful physical reactions when it finally occurred.

In our seminars and trainings we have observed that when asked how something felt people often respond by telling us what they thought. It almost always seems as if they are more comfortable talking about thoughts than feelings.

Uncommunicated Feelings

If you have a feeling about something and do not tell anyone about it, what happens to it? Does it just disappear from your consciousness? It's probably fair to say that no one can give a definitive scientific answer to those questions. But it is reasonable to suggest that the feelings we have in reaction to events that have emotional impact on us are not forgotten. If they are not forgotten and not communicated to someone else, it's likely that we are somehow storing the memories of those feelings inside our bodies.

When we bypass our natural ability to communicate what we feel, we develop the bad habit of using our bodies as storage tanks rather than processing plants. Now let's add the fact that we also learn to limit the communication of some of our thoughts and ideas as well as our feelings. We learn that sad, painful, or negative thoughts are not well received, so we store them too. We then start to build up a collection of uncommunicated thoughts and feelings that clog up our memories and make it difficult for us to participate fully in life.

We Express Only Happy Feelings

When something affects us emotionally, we want to tell the people who are important to us. If you get a promotion at work, you will generate a lot of emotional energy about it. Usually, you'd immediately call someone and tell them. If you have to work all day and don't have a chance to share it right away, at the end of the day you'll tell the good news to your family and friends. When you do talk about it, you'll probably reexperience the feelings you had when you first got the notification. It's also likely that you'll keep thinking and talking about it for at least a few days. Telling others your positive feelings is easy. Almost always, the people in your life are eager for you to share your excitement and happiness with them. And it's unlikely that anyone will say, "Don't feel good," in response to your happy news.

You also have a natural desire to share your sad feelings with others. If you got passed over for a promotion, you would undoubtedly be disappointed. Your first instinct might be to call someone and tell them. We said "might" because you may have learned that it's not safe to tell others your sad feelings, because they might say, "Don't feel bad, you'll get it next time." It may or may not be true that you will someday get the promotion, but the real issue is that you do feel bad, and you feel bad right now. What may happen the next time is not what you are concerned about. The fact that you don't feel safe to talk openly about those feelings doesn't mean that those feelings cease to exist, so you must store them inside your body.

We Learn to Store Feelings

Our earliest attempts at romance did not last forever, so we probably stored some sad emotions after they ended. That's why we spent so much time in the opening chapter talking about the ideas we learned early in life about dealing with sad feelings. As a result of practicing those ideas, we create a feeling filter that inhibits us from talking about our feelings. It has been suggested that those feelings wind up in the same place as all the missing socks. That would be funny if the issue wasn't so life limiting. So where do those feelings go? If you really want to know, put this book down and go look in a mirror. Look from your throat all the way down to your stomach. That's where your uncommunicated emotions are stored.

When a romantic relationship ends, there are feelings and thoughts that you need to discuss. If you're like most people, you learned all of those six myths we exposed in the first chapter. In the crisis caused by the end of a relationship, your own head will tell you **don't feel bad**; **replace the loss**; **grieve alone**; **time heals**; **be**

strong; and **keep busy**. Your mind will deliver those six ideas up at lightning speed, along with any others it believes will help you deal with the feelings you're having. With those ideas as your guidelines, you'd be inclined to put a lid on the communication of your sad feelings. Instead of telling the people in your life how you feel, you will act as if you're fine, when nothing could be further from the truth.

If your sad feelings persist, you may hear this phrase: "It's been X amount of time, you should be over it by now." You may even be saying it to yourself. It is most likely that you will continue to bury the recurring sad feelings inside your body in an attempt to show that you can be strong. It seems right to do that because the information you learned over your lifetime indicates that feeling sad is bad and shouldn't be shared with others.

We've met many people who have been holding on to feelings about important life events for decades. This happens despite the human system being perfectly designed to process and communicate all our feelings in real time. When we trap feelings inside our bodies, there are emotional and physical consequences. Like tiny time bombs, they can come back to haunt us when we least expect it.

Stored Feelings Produce Energy

Without getting scientific, we think you'll agree that emotions trapped inside our bodies create energy.

However, individual feelings do not exist as specific, concrete, and locatable elements inside your body. While the idea that feelings can somehow exist inside us is more than a metaphor, they won't show up on an x-ray. Even so, undelivered emotional communications, either positive or negative, remain inside us until they are spoken out loud to another person.

Your Emotional Boiling Point

The uncommunicated feelings stored inside your body cook until they reach an emotional boiling point. Envision the middle of your body as a teakettle. Think about how a teakettle works. You fill it with water, put it on the stove, light the burner, and then wait for the water to boil. As the water inside reaches the boiling point, the buildup of energy causes a whistle to escape from the hole in the top of the kettle to notify you that the water has boiled. Now imagine the inside of your body, jam-packed with the feelings you've never communicated. Many have been in there for a long time, and over time your body will cook them in much the same way a teakettle heats water. As the pressure mounts inside, our bodies try to notify us. Unfortunately, we don't always hear the warning. By the time we become aware that we have built up so much energy, we usually do not consciously connect it to the events that caused those feelings in the first place. The emotions we store make the potential for relationship happiness more and more remote.

Short-Term Energy Relieving Behaviors

A short-term energy relieving behavior (STERB) is anything we do to try to release the emotional energy that builds up in our bodies. A STERB is also any activity we participate in that gives us the *illusion of relief* from what we feel. The most obvious and common STERB is the use of food. "Don't feel bad; here, have a cookie" starts us on this path very early in life. We tend to activate it each time we have an emotional crisis, even though we may not be aware that we're doing it. Some of the other most common STERBs are alcohol or drugs, anger, exercise, fantasy (TV, movies, books, Internet), isolation, sex, shopping (also called retail therapy), and workaholism. We're sure that you've used one or more from that list in an attempt to deal with the emotions you felt when a relationship ended.

The problem with STERBs is that they appear to relieve some of the pressure we feel, yet all they do is distract us from the real issues. That's why we say they create only an *illusion of relief.* They address only the buildup of energy and not what caused it in the first place. As a result there is no permanent relief. As the first two letters of the acronym indicate, there's only short-term reduction of the pressure. It's parallel to cutting off just the tops of weeds, which then grow right back. Clearly, it would make more sense to pull them out by the roots so they are gone permanently. Participating in STERBs, like cutting the weeds, must be done over and over, since the real issue that caused the buildup of energy is never addressed.

As our feelings cook in the teakettle example, the pressure inside our bodies mounts and creates real energy. The event that's causing us to generate so much emotional energy may have happened days, weeks, or even years ago. We might use food or other substances in an attempt to push the feelings down. This only serves to distract us temporarily. We might throw ourselves into work or play, fostering a false sense of well-being because we are so busy. We might dive into books, movies, television, or our computers well beyond the normal needs for pleasant diversion. As with the use of substances or keeping busy, escapism only fosters the illusion that we're dealing with the mounting feelings. Again, none of those activities directly address the feelings and thoughts caused by the original event.

Over time those short-term activities often become habits that hide the underlying issues. If someone hurts our feelings and we eat a quart of ice cream over it, we haven't dealt with the feelings about the hurt, but we've consumed an awful lot of calories. If we do that kind of thing too often, our weight and other health issues replace the hurt feelings as the presenting problem. In the meantime, no matter how much ice cream we eat, the uncommunicated emotions are still stuck inside our bodies.

Negative Consequences of STERBs

There are long-term negative consequences to our emotional and physical health when we use STERBs. To one degree or another, we all try to dispel emotional energy with STERBs. However, when a STERB becomes a habit, it becomes the problem and over-shadows the original event that caused us to activate the STERB. Nowhere is this more obvious than in our reactions to the emotions caused by the end of romantic relationships.

STERBS Create False Emotional Protection

If you use shopping to make yourself feel good, the credit card bills will bring with them a new problem that removes the original emotional event from view. STERBs do nothing to complete what is left emotionally unfinished. At best, a STERB can release a little of the energy stored inside your body. At worst, there can be major consequences that create problems that push your broken heart entirely out of the picture.

Rather than creating emotional protection, the use of STERBs usually causes us to try to protect ourselves by being less honest about our emotions. This will sabotage any new relationship we might enter. We've talked to thousands of people about this, and more than 95 percent of them have told us that emotional honesty is what they want most from their mates. One of the phrases you hear a lot today is that someone wasn't "emotionally available." Sadly, many of the people who complained about a former romantic partner being unavailable didn't realize that they weren't either. They were not aware of their own part until they recognized that many of the STERBs they brought with them into the relationship were the result of incompleteness in prior relationships. They weren't really emotionally available either.

STERBs Hurt Our Bodies

Using STERBs to deal with stored feelings can make your body malfunction. The physical consequences range from minor to grave. Once they start, they dominate your attention and push the original issues out of sight. When that happens, it's difficult to go back and deal with the original emotional events that caused them.

One of the most obvious results of not dealing effectively with feelings is the increase of tension. It has spawned an entire industry devoted to massaging away the daily buildup of stress that accumulates within us. Many people feel that tension in their necks, some in the chest or stomach. Your body will find its weakest link, and that's where it will break down when the pressure builds up. If your back is your trouble spot, then it will crumple. If you're predisposed to heart problems, continued emotional pressure can activate them. The modern diagnosis of irritable bowel syndrome has become almost epidemic and is typical of what can happen when we store emotions. Many of the medical conditions we experience are brought on when we don't process our feelings effectively. Once those conditions emerge, they become the presenting issues and must be dealt with medically. At that point, concerns about the relationships that have ended are pushed further out of sight while we deal with our health.

Emotional Explosions

When the accumulation of emotions inside our bodies achieves critical mass, we're liable to explode. Like most people, you've probably stored a lot of feelings about relationships that have ended. Think about what would happen if you added another romantic ending to that combustible mixture. Undoubtedly it would ratchet up the pressure inside you to the highest levels, but your belief system would still tell you to keep a lid on it and not tell others. The effect is like the teakettle with a high flame under it but with no spout to release the steam or whistle a warning. Your body is no different. If you apply enough heat for enough time and then add one more emotional event, the pressure inside will be more than you can tolerate. An explosion is inevitable. If you've ever wondered why you have exploded, now you know. It's the direct result of using your body as an emotional storage tank.

As you read this, you might also realize that there were times that you and your former mate blew up at the same time. What a mess! Take two human teakettles jammed to the brim with a lifetime collection of undelivered emotions, add the emotions generated by an argument, and you have all the ingredients for an explosion.

Holding On to Feelings Drains Energy

Holding on to feelings consumes much more energy than communicating them. It's exhausting to drag the baggage along everywhere you go. You may now understand why you've felt exhausted for long stretches following a breakup. You may also realize that you made some very poor decisions while your teakettle was busy cooking up the feelings you'd stored. Although you may not have been consciously aware of what was brewing inside you, it probably took its toll on your ability to concentrate and function. Your life works better when you process your feelings in the moment they occur, rather than storing them.

Overload Leads Back to STERBs

As your body gets overloaded with an accumulation of emotions, you will engage more and more in your STERBs. You have to keep doing them as the pressure keeps mounting. Eventually, the STERBs will even stop having the short-term benefit of distracting you. The illusion of well-being they have given you will stop working. But since you have taken no actions to complete what was emotionally unfinished in your just-ended relationship, the pressure will keep building.

Some people think that one way to avoid the buildup of emotional energy is to talk about what they are feeling. But you must be careful and realize that talking about your feelings will not automatically help you avoid explosions or stop using STERBs. There's a danger in believing that just talking about feelings is all you need to do. We all know people who talk about their painful feelings in what seems like an endless loop. For them, talking about their feelings becomes a STERB. They are the people you sometimes avoid because they tell the same sad story over and over. When you see people like that, you realize that just talking about how you feel doesn't mean that you will never create any baggage to drag forward.

Talking about how you feel is good to a limited degree, but it doesn't complete your relationship to the emotions caused by the end of a relationship. Talking about the same feelings over and over compares to taking aspirin every time your head hurts but never investigating the cause of the headache. What you must learn are the actions that will help you complete your relationship to the painful events that have caused you to feel bad.

STERBs and Habits Specific to Romantic Endings

In a crisis we go back to our oldest beliefs and behaviors. We'll automatically begin to indulge the STERBs we use most often. At the same time, the habits we've developed in reaction to loss will also kick in. One of the most common habits following a breakup is the attempt to replace the loss. People rush out and begin dating someone new while they still have an arrow sticking out of their hearts. Talk about bringing baggage into a new relationship! But it makes sense when you realize that for most of us the idea of replacing the loss is one of our oldest learned ideas. Some people even activate the habit of replacing the loss in advance of the end of a relationship, when they see it's going downhill. They start collecting phone numbers and sending out signals. It's obvious that those kinds of actions in no way deal directly with the feelings they have about the relationship that's about to end.

"Replace the loss" is a habit that's learned early in life and gets used many times along the way. Let us illustrate by connecting the little girl from the preschool story to that same girl ten years later as a teenager, and then to her as a young woman of twenty-five. When her preschool classmates told her they didn't want to be her friends anymore, her parents told her not to feel bad and to go make new friends. When she was fifteen, a boy she had been seeing told her he didn't want to go out with her anymore. It's very likely that she heard the same line as Russell had in a similar situation: "Don't feel bad, there are plenty of fish in the sea." And at age twenty-five, after a broken engagement, she may have heard, "Don't feel bad, there are plenty more where he came from." By now, you'll recognize the last part of that comment as just another variation on "replace the loss." Put the three together, and there is a strong likelihood that she will push her sad feelings down into her body and begin the replacement search right away. To compound this, there will be many friends and allies lined up to help her find new recruits.

In addition to practicing replace the loss, this little girl/teenager/young woman has probably used food or other distractions to deal with painful emotions. It's likely that she now has some habits, which we would call STERBs, that she uses when she feels bad. In the crisis caused by her latest breakup, she will use one or more STERBs in trying to deal with her emotions. She will also use any other ideas she's learned to deal with her sad feelings as she reels under the emotional weight of the breakup. She might try to be strong in an attempt to hide her feelings so others will not judge her as weak. She may throw herself into a whirlwind of activity, using the idea of keeping busy to distract herself from what she is feeling. Doesn't sound like this will lead anywhere good, does it?

When all indirect attempts to deal with her feelings fail, she may give up dating altogether and become cynical about ever finding happiness.

Anger from Past Affects Future

Anger is one of the more common STERBs for people who have trash-compacted their emotions inside their bodies. When a relationship is sliding downhill, there's a strong probability that feelings will be stored and anger will be generated. When the relationship ends, anger may escalate dramatically. This can really be limiting when you try to build a new relationship that is based on emotional honesty.

How People Use STERBs

Here are a couple of real-life examples of how people use STERBs. You might identify with one or both, and it will show you that you're not alone in seeking short-term relief.

The Ice Cream Cure

Our friend Jane told us of her attempt to use ice cream to cure her broken heart. After four years of bickering and reconciling, she and Todd called it quits. Although she was relieved that the battles were over, she was left with an overwhelming feeling of emptiness. On the third night after the breakup, she found herself heading for the freezer. Her head said, "I need comfort food," so she decided that ice cream would fill the bill. That night she consumed a pint of mint chocolate chip. The next night she ate a quart of rocky road. The more depressed she felt about Todd, the more she turned to ice cream. Soon she no longer bothered with a bowl and just ate right out of the container.

During the next few months she put on ten pounds and didn't even care. But that was just one of the consequences. The sense of comfort she got each night from eating the ice cream became the only thing she was interested in. But the comfort was short-lived, and the next day she was racked with remorse about what she'd done the night before. Her sad feelings reappeared and she started the cycle again. Some time each day she'd be overcome with an absolute belief that she would never be happy in a relationship. That of course triggered her to head back to the freezer and start the loop one more time.

Brent Went from Alcohol to Videos

Brent's story is interesting and a little bit unusual. He instigated the ending of the relationship and then was devastated when Mary agreed. He told us, "I think I asked for the breakup as a way of trying to getting Mary to change. Somehow I believed that if she could be different, the relationship would get better. I badgered her, trying to get her to go to therapy or to try meditation, anything. The more I pushed, the more she pulled away. When I asked for the ending, she was gone in a shot."

After the breakup, Brent started having several drinks every night to dull the pain. For a while it seemed to work. He'd drink enough to make himself forget how he felt. The mornings were a little rough, but it seemed like a small price to pay for the relief of not having to deal with the emotions that were tearing him apart. But after a few months, the drinking didn't work anymore. He started renting movies and sat in his darkened den every night, watching one movie after another. Even though he was distracted by the films, when he got into bed each night, the hole in his heart remained.

Exercise 2: Identifying Your STERBs

It's time to look at what you've been doing to try to deal with your feelings. We'll go first and tell you that we've each used a variety of STERBs to deal with the breakups and divorces that affected our lives. Since athletics were such a large part of John's young life, he would spend many hours practicing the sports he loved. Of course there were benefits in enhancing his abilities in the games he played, but it did nothing to repair the pain caused by romantic endings. Russell tended to isolate himself and would sit for hours at pinball machines (in today's world he would have been the king of video games). But that skill also did nothing to help Russell deal with the emotions he had experienced or to reduce the fear he had of getting hurt again.

As they got older, they each found other STERBs. John used alcohol to the point that it overtook his life.

He had to stop drinking altogether just to stay alive. Russell got into reading mystery and spy novels. He spent every nonworking minute immersed in the lives of the heroes and villains he read about.

It's time to get out your notebook again. We have listed some of the most common STERBs to help you recognize some of the behaviors you've used to deal with sad feelings no matter what caused them. We want you to look at our list and then write down the ones that you've used. Then add any that are not on our list. Here's our list to get you started:

food
alcohol or drugs
anger
exercise
sex
fantasy (music, movies, TV, books, computer)
isolation
shopping (also called retail therapy)
workaholism

After you've written down all of your STERBs, think about the ones you used most when your romantic relationships ended. Circle them on your list. As you think about this and write some things down, please don't be critical of yourself or your behavior. After you finish, put your notebook in a safe and private place.

CHAPTER FOUR

YOU'RE RESPONSIBLE FOR YOUR FEELINGS

The suggestion that you're responsible for your feelings might be an obvious statement, but just knowing that may not be enough. That awareness doesn't mean that you've been able to avoid the pitfall of assigning responsibility for your feelings to others. In countless relationship endings, the problems began with one or both of the partners misunderstanding emotional responsibility. With very few exceptions, both partners in failed relationships assigned the blame for their feelings to the other person. As a result, neither was ever willing to look at their own part. Such thinking creates a victim mentality, which causes so many relationships to be unsuccessful. And worse, it makes completion of prior relationships impossible, therefore creating the failure of the next relationship in advance.

Now we need to address the issue of responsibility for having the feelings in the first place. You might be asking, "But what if my mate said or did something really hurtful?" Our reply remains the same. You are responsible for your feelings even if you believe that the words or actions of someone else may have initially caused them. As hard as it is to believe, even if the other person apologized to you for what they had done, you would still be saddled with your reaction to it. It is you who sustains the resentment and drags your feelings forward as emotional baggage.

The false idea that others have the power to make us feel is instilled in childhood. It's not intentional. Rather, it's part of the multigenerational pass-through of incorrect information that happens even in the healthiest of homes. As with other things we've highlighted in this book, the situations in which we originally learned things may not always seem to have a direct correlation to romantic relationships. Yet, when we examine them closely, we see that many of the things we learned long ago come back to haunt us at the very time we need better information.

Life Lessons at the Dinner Table

It probably won't surprise you when we say that much of what you believe—good and bad—you learned at the dinner table. When we were young most of us heard things such as "Don't do that, you'll make your father angry" or "Your good report card makes Mommy feel proud." On the surface those comments seem harmless. But viewing them under an emotional microscope exposes the breeding grounds for one of the largest relationship problems: the placement of responsibility for your feelings. How that actually happens may surprise you. When adults say, "You make me feel," it teaches children that their actions cause the adults to feel something. It suggests that the adult is not responsible for his or her feelings. Even worse, it teaches the child that he is also not responsible for his own feelings.

A child who hears "Don't do that, you'll make your daddy angry" will come home from school with his own version of that. He will have an interaction that got him in trouble, and his defense will be "I did it because Jimmy made me mad." It's a simple formula: if I can make Daddy angry, then Jimmy can make me angry. And none of it's my fault or my responsibility because "he made me mad." When we're socialized to believe that others cause us to feel, it becomes our default setting. **The reality is that we are 100 percent responsible for our reactions to the things other people say or do.** But when there's a problem, we'll automatically search our belief system to see what information we have about the thoughts and feelings we're having. That is when we will apply the idea that someone else causes us to feel and we'll hold them 100 percent responsible.

Elizabeth's Breakup—Misplaced Responsibility

To show you what can happen when we place responsibility for our feelings outside ourselves, here's how easily we can divert ourselves from the real issues. Elizabeth kept telling her sad story with a total focus on the fact that Kevin announced he was leaving her three days before Christmas. She was staggered. She believed that his doing it at that time was totally responsible for the devastation she felt. She told us that she was so self-righteous about his timing that she completely overlooked the fact that the relationship had been declining for a long time.

With her focus totally on *how* and *when* the ending happened and not *why*, she continued to make Kevin the villain. She made the way he ended the relationship exclusively responsible for how she felt. She excused herself from any responsibility for what had happened over the years they were together. From that perspective, there was no way she could get emotionally complete.

Getting Out of Emotional Jail

When you hold someone else 100 percent responsible for your feelings, you place yourself in an emotional jail. The other person can never let you out, because it's a jail of your own construction. It is built on the idea that not only do others have the power to make you feel but you must keep feeling it until they release you. We hate to be the bearer of bad news, but they're not coming to set you free. That's your job. We're not exaggerating. Think about some of the events and arguments that happened in your past romantic relationships. Think about how steadfastly your partner stuck to his or her position about who did what to whom. Think about how much energy you consumed in your belief that he or she was responsible for how you felt.

It's bad enough that we hold the other person responsible for how we feel when a relationship has ended, but the situation is inflamed when people tell us that the other person was to blame. Well-meaning people say things like, "It's not your fault; he was always so rigid." The comment about it not being your responsibility is almost always followed by an example of what the other person did wrong. With that kind of input, we rarely take responsibility for anything we did within the relationship. Nor do we take responsibility for the feelings we had when the relationship ended. We tend to blame the other person for what happened and how we feel. It is all part of a victim mentality that keeps us blind to our part. It also removes us from responsibility for having chosen to be with or stay with that person. This victim mentality didn't happen by accident, nor did it first happen at the time of your latest breakup. The wheels were set in motion a long time ago.

The only truth is that you are responsible for all the feelings you've had in reaction to what your mates have said or done. Why? Because it is the only thing you can work on. For the moment, allow yourself to think only about your part. How often did you feel as if he or she made you feel something? You don't have to drag out your notebook and make a formal exercise out of this yet, but we really want you to think about that question. Be as honest as you can about your part. It'll help you as you do the next exercise and will enable you to take more responsibility for your feelings in future romantic relationships.

You're Also Responsible for Your Intuition

You're as responsible for your willingness to follow your intuition as you are for the feelings you have in reaction to people and events. If you can accept that you're responsible for your emotional reactions, then it follows that you must accept that you're responsible for following your intuition. This is crucial, because when you fail to follow your intuitive sense as you date and begin a relationship, the consequences are usually major.

Intuition Is an Early Warning System— Overlook It at Your Peril

Your intuition is the most accurate indicator of what is good and right for you. It gives you almost immediate and accurate early warning information. Unfortunately, your intuition may have gotten lost at the same time you were being influenced to believe that others were responsible for how you feel. We've interacted with thousands of people who came to us because of one or more broken relationships. We've asked them individually and in groups if there had been a point when they knew that the person they were with wasn't right for them. It probably won't surprise you to learn that many of them knew long before the ending that it wasn't going to work out. Most of them knew before the relationship was formalized in any way, but they chose to stay and stayed until the inevitable ending. By then, the cumulative damage was much greater than it might have been had they ended the relationship when they first knew.

We can tell you that about 80 percent of the people we've helped told us that they'd overruled their intuition in one or more relationships. As a result, they caused themselves (and others) tremendous emotional damage by entering or staying in relationships they knew couldn't work out. Usually they knew very early on. The common denominator was that they all stayed much too long after they knew, thus compounding the pain and making it more and more difficult to exit the relationship. Since 80 percent is a pretty compelling number, we can safely guess that most of you reading this book have done the same.

The Role of Compromise

We're often asked if it's true that compromise is an important element of successful romantic relationships. Our answer is a thundering *yes*! We're also asked if it's true that you have to work at relationships, that love alone is not enough to create success. Again, the answer is *yes*! But the crucial question does not relate to compromise or hard work, it relates to that intuitive sense of whether you belong with that person. If you don't belong together, that's the one thing that cannot be compromised. It's the one thing that all the work in the world cannot overcome.

Since most of us learned to distrust our intuition a long time ago, it makes it hard to tune into it when we need it. For the moment, we're going to ask you to think about your intuition and, specifically, about whether you have bypassed it when entering romantic relationships. No need to get out your notebook just yet, but let your mind wander back over the relationships you've been in. Think about what you knew and when you knew it. The more honest you can be about yourself, the better the chances of completing past relationships and avoiding the same pitfalls in the future.

Self-Sabotage Begins with You

As you look at the issues we're addressing, you might see that you've been at least a partial architect of some

It's the one thing you can never give up; never compromise on. That's the real thing you need in love. — K. Loggins

of your disasters. Not because you're bad or because you're stupid, but because you have practiced and perfected what you were taught. The primary reason you may have seemed to sabotage a relationship that might have been the "right" one was that you incorrectly thought it would protect your emotions. If you are told not to feel bad after a breakup, but you do anyway, then you will try to avoid feeling bad again. What's the best way to avoid feeling hurt? Don't get attached to anyone emotionally! When you withhold from your partner, you are setting up the ending. The built-in sabotage is inevitable under those conditions.

Self-sabotage is usually unconscious rather than intentional. Most of us don't sit around thinking up ways to destroy our relationships. How it happens is less important than the impact it has on us when we realize that we have contributed to the ending of a relationship. We're sure that you have gone over and over the scenarios that led up to the endings of your relationships. Up until now, you may not have had the perspective you are gaining from this book. You were probably unaware that most of what you have been doing was in direct response to what you had learned and practiced for a very long time. The problem is that much of what you learned was not helpful for you. You may even have been harsh with yourself about your mistakes. The next exercise will help you discover more about your part of what has and hasn't happened in your romantic relationships.

Exercise 3: Identifying Your Part of What Went Wrong

Here's an exercise in three sections to help you discover your part of the relationships you've been in. Until you identify your part, you can't take actions to complete those relationships. Without completion you can't really do anything new and different to get better results. You will need your notebook to write down your observations in the three areas we've been discussing: emotional responsibility, intuition, and self-sabotage.

1. Others Are Responsible for How We Feel

"He made me mad," is the classic example of others making us feel something. Write down any similar comments you heard when you were young that influenced you to believe that others were responsible for how you felt. Then think about the times you thought or even said that your partner made you feel angry, sad, or frustrated. As painful as it might seem, try to remember some of the arguments you had. That might remind you that you had assigned responsibility for your feelings to the other person. Write down anything you recall that relates to making someone else responsible for how you felt. Even if you can't recall anything specific, just thinking about it will be helpful.

If nothing else, we hope you understand the idea built in to the phrase, "He made me mad." Thousands of people have reported to us that the foundational issue about who is responsible for feelings negatively affected their relationships. As long as you hold others responsible for how you feel, you will stay stuck forever.

2. Overriding Intuition

We want you to think back about some of the relationships you've been in and see if you can recall when you "knew" that it wasn't right for you, but you plowed on anyway. It may have partially been because you had been taught that you have to work or compromise to be successful in relationships. But that's not the issue here. We just want you to see if you knew that the relationship was not going to work but you went ahead anyway.

If you believe that you bypassed your intuition at any time in any of your relationships, write it down. See if you can recall how early in the relationship it happened. Make notes of the ideas you used to justify going ahead. Be as honest as you can. This is a crucial area and honesty about it now may help you in the future.

3. Self-Sabotage

The most common reason that people sabotage relationships is because they're trying to protect themselves from getting hurt again. This happens when we don't know how to complete the pain caused when relationships end. We want you to think about your prior romantic relationships with the idea that your fear of getting hurt again may have limited you in being open and honest in a subsequent relationship. Stay focused on your part and not that of your former partner. If you have a sense of having caused some of the problems that led to the ending of a relationship, write it down. Be as specific as you can about what you did, whether you did it consciously or not. Although you may not have realized what you were doing at the time, as you reflect on it, you may see your part now.

After you finish, put your notebook in a safe and private place.

CHAPTER

FIVE

WE SAY WE'RE FINE WHEN WE'RE NOT

When John wrote his first book on dealing with loss, he created an imaginary prize category that he labeled Academy Award Recovery. That's when people are constantly saying, "I'm fine," when that's the furthest thing from the truth. Imagination aside, the feelings that people have following painful losses are very real. The "I'm fine" lie develops when people tell the truth about how they feel in response to losses and then are told they shouldn't feel that way. Each time that happens, they feel judged for feeling bad. Since nobody ever likes to feel judged, people learn very quickly to hide their real feelings.

It's now more than twenty years since John first penned those words about Academy Award Recovery.

When he wrote that phrase, he had no idea how many people would identify with the idea contained in the metaphor. Every time we talk or write about it, people tell us that the idea of Academy Award Recovery maintains a very high identification factor in their perceived need to hide sad or painful feelings. We would love to report that the world has changed. We would love to tell you that it is now safe for you tell the truth when you have sad or painful feelings. We'd love to, but we won't. If we did, we'd be lying.

Four Questions that Explain the Problem

Here's a four-part sequence of questions we ask when addressing large groups of people and the responses they typically give:

Part 1: "How many of you like being lied to?"

Not one hand goes up.

Part 2: "How many of you have ever lied when asked, 'How do you feel?'"

More than 95 percent of the people raise their hand in response.

(Big pause here, while the people look around at how many hands are raised, then we add, "Seems like none of you like being lied to, yet nearly every one of you lies about your feelings.")

Part 3: "How many of you usually know that someone is lying to you about how they feel?"

Again, nearly every hand in the audience goes up.

(We then ask this somewhat rhetorical question, "If you usually know when others are lying, doesn't it follow that they know when you're lying?")

Part 4: "It doesn't feel good when you sense that you are being lied to, does it?"

Almost everyone in the audience shakes their head no.

(Again we slip in an obvious question, "It doesn't feel good when the roles are reversed, does it?")

Now ask yourself those questions. There's a very high probability that your answers will be the same as most of the people we've asked.

Let's put this little quiz into context. People who are dealing with the emotional aftermath of a romantic breakup have a need and a desire to talk about **what happened**. They also need and want to talk about the relationship that just ended. But having felt judged by the comments they heard after the breakup, they start lying about how they feel. This is a direct invitation to store feelings and a blueprint for an emotional explosion somewhere down the line.

We have no doubt that you have experienced one or more heartbreaking romantic endings. We know that most of you tried talking about your feelings to people you thought you could trust, only to be told something like, "Don't feel bad, another bus will be along soon." We are positive that you can relate to having tried to act recovered to keep from hearing those kinds of comments. We also know that after a while you probably tried not to tell or show people how you felt. Finally, we know that the feelings trapped inside you have been added to the baggage that makes it almost impossible for you to do anything differently and therefore get better results.

Resignation Masquerades as Acceptance

Many people tell us that they have achieved acceptance in regard to relationships that have ended. But after some honest conversation, they begin to realize that what they had achieved might better be called resignation. Acceptance is a concept that has risen in popularity as our language has become more and more psychologized. It has come to signify that someone is finished with a prior relationship and is ready to move on. Unfortunately, that is not usually the case. The problem is that people won't take real actions to complete past relationships when they labor under the idea that they've arrived at acceptance. What they don't realize is that acceptance of a situation isn't equal to being complete with the emotional impact caused by the end of the relationship.

With a little more digging, most people discover that they have buried the unfinished business from the previous relationship out of sight, not realizing that it would come back to haunt them. It's unlikely that anyone does that on purpose. It's usually the result of not having been taught how to effectively complete relationships that have ended or changed. Resignation is the indirect result of trying to move on without taking any real actions to complete the relationship that ended. There's a world of difference between completion and resignation.

In the past, we might have used the idea of acceptance to define a position from which you could begin to think about dating again with an eye toward finding a life mate. But over the years, we've come to realize that acceptance can be a confusing word and doesn't really indicate that someone is emotionally complete with past relationships. Without such completion, the baggage just gets dragged through successive relationships.

Getting Over versus Getting Complete

Another concept that confuses people who are trying to reenter the world of relationships is the idea of getting over a relationship that has ended. **The problem is that getting over implies forgetting**. The reality is that you cannot forget anyone who was important to you. The fact that you remember people who have affected your life doesn't mean that you haven't gotten over them. It also doesn't necessarily mean that you are emotionally complete with them. It simply means that you remember them and the important things in your relationships with them.

To get emotionally complete, you're going to have to change some of your beliefs about what certain things mean. The notion of "getting over" is another idea you must discard. When you continue to have sad feelings about a person you're no longer with, people will suggest that you haven't gotten over that person. Not true. If it were, then when you have a fond memory and smile, it would also mean you haven't gotten over that person. A breakup does not cancel your memories about the events that happened in the relationship. Our feelings about those memories are neither good nor bad, they just are.

There's a difference between *completing* your relationship to unrealized hopes, dreams, and expectations and *forgetting* someone who was very important in your life. The first is possible, the second isn't. Using the phrase *getting over* is a setup for failure, since you cannot forget.

Moving On

As we conclude part I we want to mention one of those clichés that we're sure you heard many times when relationships ended: "Let go and move on" or variations on that theme. It sounds good, but in the end it's very bad advice. First of all, what does it mean? Let go of what and move on to where? Second, how do I let go of something that was emotionally important to me and where will I wind up if I do? Third, if I have fond memories from the relationship, will I lose them as I become complete with the painful ones? Those questions are exactly what is not addressed in "Let go and move on."

What you may now realize is that a part of what you've been holding on to is all the misinformation you've acquired about dealing with loss in the first place. As you become more aware of how you have been dealing with the feelings associated with romantic endings, you will finally be able to complete what was emotionally unfinished in prior relationships. You then have the real possibility of moving on and finding a relationship that is right for you. As we proceed, we will help you see specifically what you must do to move on. You will be able to keep fond memories without them turning painful. You will be able to become complete with everything that was emotionally unfinished for you so that you will not drag it along as emotional baggage.

PART II

Small and Correct Choices

Completion of prior relationships is achieved by a series of small and correct choices. You have already made several choices and taken action on them. By reading this far in the book and doing the early exercises you have done the following:

You have acknowledged that a problem exists.

You have acknowledged that the problem is associated with incomplete past relationships.

You have acknowledged that you are willing to take action to complete your past so you can start anew.

In doing the exercises in the earlier chapters, you started taking actions based on what is true for you. While this is a good beginning, there's more to do. We're now going to ask you to start digging a little deeper.

CHAPTER SIX

TRUTH ALONE DOESN'T SET YOU FREE

There's a famous expression, "Know the truth and the truth will set you free." As well known and accepted as that phrase may be, it is flawed. The flaw is not in what is said but in what is omitted. While paying respect to the original idea, we would like to enhance the expression and make it more practical for you.

Discover the truth,
take action based on the truth,
the result will set you free.

The key word in our definition is *action*. Without new action there can be no freedom of choice. Without new action you will continue to practice the old habits that caused you so much relationship pain in the first place. Here's a question and some comments about it that illustrate how telling the truth doesn't always set people free. Have you ever known someone who tells the same painful story of a relationship gone bad, over and over? Though the story may be truthful, it does nothing for the teller other than to confirm the pain he or she feels. The constant recitation of a painful story, usually accompanied by a diatribe against the former partner, does nothing to encourage the storyteller to do anything different the next time.

When you think of people you've known who tell those stories, it might conjure up the image of a hamster on a wheel, going round and round. We're sure that you've wanted to help your friends get off that wheel, but try as you might, they keep going in circles. Their pain, and the story they tell, becomes their identity.

Truth is like time in the sense that they both exist but neither can actually do anything, because they are not actions.

The key to change is to take new actions within time that are based on what is true for you.

Romantic Relationship History

You can't become emotionally complete with your past until you are clear about what it is. To help you get an accurate picture, we're going to have you take a look at your romantic relationship history. We're sure that you're familiar with the phrase "history repeats itself." This is especially true in romantic relationships, where you're most likely to repeat past mistakes in future relationships. As you look openly at what has happened since your earliest attempts at relationships, there's a strong probability that you'll see some of the habits you've developed.

For most people, the romantic relationship history begins at the onset of puberty. That's when young minds shift from ballet or baseball to hormonally driven matters. Many of those early relationships aren't even real but are the stuff fantasies are made of. Almost every young girl and boy develops crushes. Often the object of that affection is a "larger than life" public figure. We've rarely met anyone who didn't recall having a crush on a rock star or movie star or some other famous person. And most can recall that their heart was at least a little bit broken when their fantasy star married someone other than them. "Why didn't they wait for me?" Even though it sounds silly, it's how our youthful hearts react. Before we've begun our own fledgling attempts at love with one of our contemporaries, we've usually had at least one or more of those fantasy relationships. This remains true through all generations.

As a seventh grader, age twelve, Russell remembers having an overwhelming crush on an "older woman," his English teacher. She was probably about twenty-five years old. Russell remembers thinking that she was the most beautiful woman in the world. That fantasy marks the beginning of Russell's personal relationship history, which appears below. Later you'll see John's relationship history.

Russell's Romantic Relationship History

1955	Miss Barrows*
1956	Denise
1956	Karen
1957	Carol
1958	Linda
1959	Brenda
1960	Mary
1961	Stacy
1964	Susan
1968	Vivienne
1974	Jeanne
1987	Alice

Russell's list includes some very early romances in high school that had emotional significance for him but

---

* Fantasy relationships must be completed also. It is not uncommon for people to arrive at our doorstep with a long list of unhappy endings. For many, hidden beneath that accumulation is a fantasy mate. The fantasy partner is one who has been created and fine-tuned over a long time. Because they are not real, these fantasy men and women are flawless. There's no way a real flesh and blood person can compete against a dream. Some people have to complete their relationships with their fantasy man or woman so they can accept the real person who has entered their life.

wouldn't really qualify as full-fledged relationships. He put them in his history because, in looking at them, something important was revealed to him about how he dealt with his emotions when each one ended. What follows is Russell's short narratives about the relationships that appear on his list.

1955—I was twelve years old. My English teacher, Miss Barrows, was the first "relationship" that I remember. It was pure fantasy. When Miss Barrows got married, I was crushed. **I didn't tell anyone how I felt.**

1956—I was infatuated with a girl named Denise. I was able to talk to her only a few times. Visions of Denise would dance in my brain and make concentrating on schoolwork almost impossible. I wanted to ask her out, but I was afraid. When I saw her holding hands with another boy, I was crushed. When I expressed how badly I felt, my friends told me, **"Don't feel bad;** *she wasn't right for you." That comment didn't help me at all.*

1956–1960—During my high school years I dated Karen, Carol, Linda, Brenda, and Mary. While each of them might qualify as minirelationships, the one that hurt the most was the very first one with Karen. I was thirteen and fourteen while we were going steady. She was my first love. After it ended I was broken-hearted. When I told my family and friends how I felt, they said things like, "Don't feel bad; you'll do better next time." But at that point—the ripe old age of fourteen—I didn't want a "next time." I hurt too much. That may have been the last time I trusted people with my hurt feelings. **From then on, I just kept the hurt inside.**

The next year, when I started seeing Carol, I remember being very careful. I did not want a repeat of getting hurt. So I was much less forthcoming with my feelings. In the end she said, "It looks like you don't seem to care." I did care, but I was unwilling to take the risk and show it. **I didn't tell anyone how I felt.** *I just tried to stay cool and pretend that it didn't bother me, but it did.*

The other relationships during the high school years opened and closed the same way. The more I tried to protect myself from the kind of pain I'd felt before, the more I withheld my feelings. Because of my withholding, they were all doomed from the start.

1961—In my first year of college I met Stacy. We hit it off very well. For a while, caught up in the passion and excitement, I forgot about protecting my heart, as I'd been doing for years. But after the first few arguments, I started pulling back, fearful of getting hurt again. When the relationship crashed and burned, I was devastated and swore that I'd never let myself get hurt again. As was now my custom, **I kept it all to myself.**

The next few years were a blur. I didn't date much. I used sports as one of my major STERBs to deal with the energy I felt about being unattached. I dated a little but was unwilling to make any emotional connection.

1964—In my senior year, a mutual friend introduced me to Susan. I asked her out. That began a rocket ride that went up with exhilarating emotions and plans of marriage only to come down to earth a few months later in a fiery heap. That ending was just a few weeks before college graduation. Cast adrift, and in keeping with my habit, **I didn't talk to anyone about what I was feeling.**

After graduating, much of my time was devoted to learning how to support myself and developing a career. I'd gotten into the restaurant business in New York and then moved to London. I dated several young women there, but as I recall, I was being very protective of my heart because of the last devastating breakup.

1968—I was running an exciting bistro in London when I met Vivienne. She was young, just nineteen, but her English accent made her seem more mature than her American counterparts. I was head over heels in love, and right away. We met on a Sunday; we got married on Tuesday. (That's not a misprint.) After that two-day engagement, we were married in the Chelsea Town Hall on King's Road in London. A few months later, we moved to Los Angeles, began our marriage, and then opened our own restaurant.

On a fateful day in 1972, it all ended in a heartbeat when I got a "sudden death" phone call. Vivienne told me that she was leaving. I had thought that we were happy—at least I was. I was stunned. I don't know how I drove a car safely in the aftermath of the divorce. And if you haven't already guessed, **I didn't talk openly about my feelings with anyone.**

After that divorce I was convinced that not only was I a failure but that I'd never be able to trust anyone again. In spite of those ideas, nature kept calling. I started dating again, **but with a renewed commitment to never again make a commitment.** After all, each time I did, I got very badly hurt.

1974—I met and married Jeanne. We were together for twelve years. Upon reflection, there were definitely some intuitive tips that I overlooked right at the outset. But we persevered. As I look back, I think we both really worked at the relationship, and we both made an awful lot of compromises, but we just didn't really belong together. For my part, I now see that the unfinished aspects of all my prior relationships brought huge burdens to that marriage. Twelve years later, after a lot of struggles, we divorced. Splitting up a life after that much time and effort, and splitting up things—even in essence having to split up friends—was difficult and painful for me.

In addition to the sadness of the ending, there was a compounding element for me. At the time of that divorce I was forty-four years old. My sense of my life and time made me feel not only like a failure again, but as if I was never going to find the lifelong relationship and companionship that my parents—and Jeanne's—had found. I was afraid that I'd never find someone to go off into the sunset with.

There was one big difference after this ending. I'd developed some friendships with people who talked more openly about emotions. They helped me feel safe enough to talk about what I felt. That same year I arrived at the Grief Recovery Institute and learned how to complete my past relationships.

1987—A mutual friend fixed me up with Alice. Here we are eighteen years later, going strong and getting better. Alice is the "one," and I really mean it this time. I'm glad I can have a little humor about this not-always-funny topic. I believe that what most helped sustain this relationship over time was the work I did to complete all the earlier ones. In emptying my little red wagon of the baggage I had dragged with me from all of my earlier relationships, I made room for a new relationship.

I don't want to make it sound like some kind of instant perfection was at play here. Indeed, Alice and I have had to work and compromise and even tolerate each other's foibles. But the one thing I can say is that my intuition was active and accurate right from the onset. Even through our occasional squabbles, I have never felt anything other than that we belonged together. I cannot predict the future, but I certainly hope it continues this way.

An Honest Examination Shows a Pattern

Russell had first written his romantic relationship history at about the time that he and Alice had begun their relationship, eighteen years ago. As a direct result of making that honest examination, Russell could see some patterns. From that emerged a new ability to see his part of the past relationships. What was profound, and what we're sure you noticed, was that nearly all of Russell's entries ended with a comment that indicated that he never talked to anyone about the emotions he experienced after each breakup. As the result of doing this work, he learned to talk about what had affected him. That first step encouraged him to take the actions that led to completion.

John's Romantic Relationship History

1957	Suzie
1960	Elizabeth
1966	Paula
1974	Marsha
1979	Connie
1980	Mary Jess

1949–1957—To some degree we are affected by the observations we made of other people's relationships when we were young. What I had seen modeled by my parents, my older brother, and my peers did not make me well equipped to participate in relationships.

*1957—My first "girlfriend" was a classmate in the eighth grade. House parties, dances, and movies were the dating activity of the day. Other than a prior embarrassing spin-the-bottle episode in the seventh grade, she was the first girl I ever kissed. As you might imagine, I was sure it must be love. I saw her every day at school. We talked for endless hours. During the summer we did not see each other as much as we had during the school year. By midsummer, we talked less often on the phone. And finally one day, I saw her walking down the main street holding hands with another boy. As I look back, I should have been able to feel the iron door of my heart slamming shut. My broken heart, along with my survive-at-any-price mind, jumped to the conclusion that all girls were untrustworthy. If I didn't want a repeat of this type of pain, **I would have to put up a brick wall around my heart.***

1960—By age sixteen, I was in high school, and sports dominated my life. Had it been left up to me, I probably would have never had a date in high school. As I recall my older brother harassed me into calling a girl I'd met. She seemed to like me so the emotional risk to me appeared to be low. As I often jokingly include in the talks I give, that first date might have been the most frightening night of my life. While writing this book, I even had to call my older brother so he could remind me where we went and what we did. When the date was over, I swore to never repeat the experience again. But thank goodness we began to date regularly. Looking back, I must say that I'm sure I was not the best boyfriend she could have had under the circumstances. My home life was a total mess. Growing up with an alcoholic father is never safe or pretty. Further, it tends to make children raised in this type of environment very wary of ever showing feelings. I actually remember thinking many times, **"Don't let anyone know how you feel because if they know, they can hurt you."**

That young woman probably saved my life, although I didn't know it at the time. She actually became my STERB. Because of her patience and kindness, she became the one and only person I told my feelings to for several years. I felt as if I had no other safe place. As is often the case, I did not know how important she had been to me until after we broke up.

After high school, although I had received several college scholarship offers, I joined the Marine Corps. She went off to college and fell in love with someone else. The "Dear John" letter broke my heart. I took the emotional pain and stuffed it down inside as I had done so many times before. This accumulation of unresolved pain stayed hidden deep inside for years. It affected most of my future relationships and friendships for years to come.

1966—I returned to the United States from Southeast Asia near the end of 1965. By then distrust of intuition was total and the brick wall around my feelings was thick and tall. I met my first wife while attending college. We met my first day on campus. Although I thought she was beautiful, she was dating another man, and so I did not call or pursue her in any way. I would see her in the student union from time to time. Occasionally we would have coffee and talk. Later I heard that she had broken up with the boyfriend and so I asked her on a date. She was a very good student and from time to time helped me with class work. She could also play pool as good as most of the men on campus. She laughed a great deal. Most important, however, was that she never gave her opinion about the war. She was smart enough to know that, although everyone is entitled to an opinion, unless you've had the experience to go with it, your opinion is of no value.

During the time we dated she became safe for me. What truth I told and what feelings I showed were only to her. After graduation, she took a job in California. She didn't discuss the California job offer with me before accepting it. When I found out about the job, I asked her to marry me just so I wouldn't lose her. I overrode my intuition because I was afraid. I now know that she didn't tell me about the job offer so that she could force the proposal. We were married for six years.

1974—I met a young woman and we began to keep company. We moved in together. We got pregnant. We got married. One of the great gifts of my life is our daughter, who was born in 1975. As I look back, I had no intuitive message or did not hear that this was not the relationship for me. So what happened? I cannot speak for her but for me the truth was that I was dragging around so much baggage from my past that it overwhelmed our marriage. We had a son who was born in 1977 but died shortly after he was born. His death was the defining event in the start of The Grief Recovery Institute. My ex-wife and I are still good friends. In fact, she and my present wife of twenty-five years are also great friends.

1979—Next followed a series of vain attempts to find lasting happiness in a relationship. I dated many women but for short periods of time. I think during this period I was starting to vaguely realize that I was not prepared to have a long-term, nurturing relationship. But of course I had no clue what to do about it.

I did have one fairly long relationship with a very nice woman during this period. And while it did not work out I think we both grew a great deal as the result of our involvement. It was after the end of this romance that I found myself sitting at the kitchen table one more time trying to figure what had gone wrong. (You are going to read a great deal about that experience in the last part of this book.)

1980—Let me close this section by saying that what I learned from that investigation and from doing the work *necessary to clear away all the debris from my heart is what enabled me to find and maintain the loving marriage that I now have. My bride and I have been together for more than a quarter of a century. I guarantee you that I finally got it right.*

Never Compare Losses

We're just about ready to give you instructions for writing out your romantic relationship history. But first, we want to clarify something very important. You must avoid the danger of comparing one relationship's end to others. Comparing losses minimizes feelings. It also suggests that you should look for someone who has a larger loss or more losses than you've had so you won't feel so bad. But that doesn't work, because all loss is experienced at 100 percent, and someone else's loss has nothing to do with yours. When your romantic relationship ends, your heart is not half-broken—it's all broken. Different relationship endings may have affected you with differing degrees of emotional intensity, but your response was always 100 percent of what you felt at the time. Of course we're aware that by the time there's a formal ending to a relationship, you may not be feeling a lot of emotion. The emotions may have happened along the way and by the end you were just eager to get away from it all.

Many people make the classic mistake of comparing how they feel on the inside to how their former partner looks on the outside. They'll also get upset when they learn their ex is dating and compare themselves to that if they're not dating yet. Either of those comparisons is self-defeating.

As you begin writing your romantic relationship history, stay focused on how you were affected when your relationships ended. Avoid comparisons to anyone else's stories so you don't minimize your feelings. And let's add one more area in which to avoid comparisons. We, Russell and John, are both men, but please believe us when we tell you that we've seen thousands of romantic relationship histories, and gender is not the issue. In fact, if we removed the names from our stories, you wouldn't necessarily be able to tell the gender of the writer. The bottom-line issues that affected both of us are the same that affect most people. After having had our hearts hurt in early relationships, we became very protective to try to keep from getting hurt again. Almost every woman we've met and helped has done the same thing. The result of that kind of protection is reduced openness and reduced trust that sabotage future relationships.

Your Romantic Relationship History

Now it's your turn to be as honest as you can in writing down the romantic relationships you remember. If they strike you as important, put them down on your list. There's no need to put down everyone you've ever

dated. If they didn't evolve into meaningful relationships, that's neither necessary nor helpful. We don't
want to set a rule based on how long you dated someone, but it may be helpful to think in terms of relationships that were exclusive or those in which you lived
together. You can also consider listing relationships that
you'd hoped would be formalized.

Instructions: You will need your notebook. Allow
yourself an hour or so of private time to focus on this
exercise. You may or may not have an emotional reaction to what you remember and write down. It would
be a good idea to have a box of tissues handy, just in
case. It's perfectly okay if you don't have an emotional
reaction; just be sure to be as honest as you can about
your part of each relationship.

Generally, it's easiest to make the list of romantic
relationships first and then write your short narratives
about each relationship. You may or may not recall the
exact year that some of your relationships began or
ended. Don't worry about those details, they're not critical. Russell and John have been doing this for a long
time so their stories are very concise. You might ram-
ble a bit as you write down your memories. Let that be
okay with you.

There's no limit as to how many relationships might
appear on your history. But be careful not to make it a
listing of everyone you ever dated. Russell listed eleven,
and John listed six. Some of you might have only one
or two relationships on your list. That's okay if it's the

truth. For you, the history might include some of the gaps where *not* having a relationship affected you. It's okay to list those gaps and to write a paragraph about what those times were like for you.

Keep the focus on you and your part of the relationships. Look back at Russell's and John's histories and see how they avoided analysis or judgment of their partners in trying to be truthful about themselves. We remind you that this is a private exercise. You are not obliged to share it with any other person. This will give you the freedom to be as truthful as possible. You will be using what you have just done very soon, so keep it handy.

Go write your romantic relationship history now.

After you finish your writing, take a few minutes and reread what you've written, without getting analytical. Let it all sink in. When you reread it, it may be emotional. Maybe not. Either way is okay. Then congratulate yourself for having done the work and put your notebook in a safe and private place.

Caution: We keep telling you to put your notebook in a safe and private place. That is always important, but now it goes to a new level. The kinds of things you are writing now must not fall into the hands of anyone else. *Do not leave your notebook where it can be found!* Some of you may be doing this work while you're involved in a romantic relationship. Be very smart. Make sure that you do not *accidentally* leave this where anyone can find it.

CHAPTER SEVEN

DISCOVERY LEADS TO COMPLETION

Discovery and completion are not the same, but you need one to accomplish the other. The romantic relationship history is a discovery action. It helps you remember your past relationships in a different way than you've ever done before. It can also expose some of your patterns and help you see your part of those relationships, which may help you determine what is emotionally unfinished for you in each of them. It would be wonderful if just listing the relationships you've been in and writing a short narrative about each one could make you emotionally complete. Unfortunately, it's not that simple. There's more to do so that you won't repeat the mistake of dragging what's incomplete from the past into your present.

As you move forward, you may have some questions. Right now, you might be wondering if you will need to complete all of the major relationships that appeared on your romantic relationship history. The answer is *yes*. But after you've done a few, you'll see that they can be done quickly and that you'll benefit greatly from doing them.

Intellectual Discovery Doesn't Complete Your Past

We're sure you've tried many ways to deal with your relationship endings. Along the way, you might have acquired a great deal of intellectual and analytical understanding about yourself. You might even be able to explain why your relationships have failed; but intellectual knowledge is of limited value. We know people who can recite a doctoral thesis on what happened and who did what to whom but still aren't emotionally complete.

Earlier we noted that at the end of a relationship, we're left with unrealized *hopes*, *dreams*, and *expectations*. But that's only half the equation you need to discover what is emotionally incomplete for you. When a relationship ends, there are always things we wish had been *different*, *better*, or *more*. Added together, those six highlighted words are the key to unlocking the puzzle that will lead you to completion. Using those ideas, we will help you discover and complete the emotions that are the primary components of your emotional baggage. It is the accumulation of unfinished emotions that makes you incomplete and causes you to hold back in successive relationships.

We're going to use a real story involving a death to illustrate how undelivered communications leave someone emotionally incomplete. It makes a powerful demonstration. Then we will show you how it correlates exactly with the unfinished emotional business that is left when a romantic relationship ends.

Bill and Jane had been married for ten years. They loved each other very much. One Sunday afternoon they went to a movie. Afterward they went to a restaurant for an early dinner. They talked about the movie and their individual reactions to it. The movie presented some very strong political ideas that stirred up emotions in both of them. As they talked, their observations turned into a heated argument. By the time their dinner arrived, they were barely talking to each other. They finished the meal in near silence and headed home. We know that's not a pretty picture, adults acting badly with each other. But we also know that most people can relate to that kind of incident.

At home the silence persisted. Neither partner was willing to apologize for their part of the argument. They went to bed without a good-night kiss and without an exchange of "I love you." They were in the same bed, just inches apart, but they might as well have been on separate planets.

When morning came, Bill got up early, showered, dressed, and left before Jane woke. On the way to work he was involved in a fatal auto accident. Jane was awakened by a call from the highway patrol with the tragic news.

The Last Night

Jane was devastated beyond words. She loved Bill, and his sudden death turned her world upside down. Her pain was compounded by that last interaction. At the funeral, all she could think about was that last night and the image of the two of them lying back to back, both stubbornly refusing to give in. This is one of those times when the words *different* and *better* crop up. You know that Jane would give anything in the world to have a chance to redo that last night with Bill.

They'd had squabbles in the past and had been able to talk things through and resolve any problems. But not this time. The last communication—or lack of it—left Jane emotionally incomplete. The accident robbed her of the chance to repair that rift. In addition, Bill's death ended the *hopes*, *dreams*, and *expectations* they had for their future together. Bill's death created emotional incompleteness in all the things that would never happen. Among many other plans, they were going to have children. That dream also died with Bill.

Instant Replay with a Different Scenario

Let's replay that situation a little differently. Using the same setup, Jane and Bill wind up facing opposite directions in the bed. Jane steams, building a case against Bill. But after a while she softens. She turns over, taps Bill on the shoulder, and whispers, "I'm sorry, honey, I think I was a little overbearing." A moment later, he turns to her and says, "No, Jane, it was me, I'm so stubborn, I'm sorry." Then, at the same moment, they both say, "I love you," and they hug and say good night. They have completed the fight. They can go to sleep and start fresh the following day.

The next morning Bill is killed in a car accident. Jane is as devastated as in the previous scenario. She will still look back over their ten years together and find things she wishes had been *different*, *better*, or *more*, and she'll find a host of unrealized *hopes*, *dreams*, and *expectations*. But she will not be emotionally incomplete with that last interaction. She will not have to replay it over and over in her mind for the rest of her life.

A Breakup Is the Death of a Relationship

We used a story involving a death to hammer home the issue of incomplete communications. What is especially poignant is that, in the first instance, Jane was left with no way to complete that incident directly with Bill. We also know that you might say that since there was a death, it's different than a romantic breakup. But the death is not the relevant issue. The parallel is that when a relationship ends—which might be called the "death" of a relationship—it's almost impossible to get emotionally complete in a direct communication with your former partner. By the time you've split up, there's so much antagonism and hurt that it's never advisable to attempt a face-to-face completion. Another problem is that the other person is not necessarily willing to talk with you. He or she may not have done the honest soul-searching it takes to be able to see and acknowledge their part of the problem. There are other reasons why completion needs to be a private action that each partner takes on his or her own. We will point them out and explain them later in this section.

The Ending Is Rarely Pleasant

The lead-up to the end of a relationship is often filled with arguments. More often than not, the last exchange a couple has is very harsh. People say hurtful things, and the breakup—like a fatal auto accident—ends the possibility of repair. That's what we mean by unfinished emotional business. The example with Jane and Bill identified only the one most obvious unfinished emotional item between them, but over the course of a ten-year marriage, there were many more.

There's always an accumulation of unfinished emotions by the time a relationship ends. You must identify and complete them before you can move forward. Until that is done, you remain emotionally incomplete. The undelivered emotional communications that you're left holding on to are the emotional baggage you drag with you. The people who've attended our workshops over the years were there because of the unfinished business left at the end of their relationships. The good news is that we were able to help them become emotionally complete. And that's exactly what we're going to show you how to do.

Who's on First

You will ultimately work on all your prior relationships. For now, the big question is, "Which one should I work on first?" Nobody can really answer that question for you. But let us give you a hint. What you brought to your most recent relationship was an accumulation of what was incomplete from your prior ones. When Russell first arrived at the Grief Recovery Institute on the heels of his second divorce, he thought that was the relationship he needed to work on. But with a little guidance from John, he chose to work on his relationship with his first wife, Vivienne. He is grateful that John pointed him in that direction, because he realized how much of what was incomplete from his first marriage had been dragged into the second one. As a result of that awareness, when he later worked on the second marriage, he was able to see his part more clearly. You might realize that you need to go back to an earlier relationship and work on it first. If so, please understand that it's normal and happens for about 60 percent of the people who do this work.

If you're still not sure which past relationship to work on first, think of these two words, *time* and *intensity*. The relationship that combined the most of those two elements may be the one to start with. But be careful, a long-term relationship with limited emotional intensity might not be the right first choice. You also have to be alert to the fact that your feelings relative to your latest breakup might still be very strong and will pull you in that direction. If you're not sure, go back and look at your narrative descriptions. The one that is the longest might indicate that it's the one you need to work on first.

Don't get preoccupied with this choice, or you'll paralyze yourself and get nothing done. As we said earlier, to get the most benefit from the actions you learn in this book, you'll need to go back and complete *all* your major relationships. Think of it this way, if you've got seven big thorns stuck in your foot, and you pull only one of them out, how much pain would you have reduced? And would you be able to walk if the other six thorns were still in there? The answers to those questions are obvious, especially the second one. You have to get *all* the thorns out.

Before you move on to the actions in the next chapter, pick the relationship that you're going to work on first.

THE ROMANTIC RELATIONSHIP REVIEW

To complete a relationship that has ended, you must review the relationship and discover what the ending left emotionally incomplete for you. That is done using three separate exercises that help you remember the most emotionally affecting events within that relationship. These are the next crucial action steps on your journey. We call it the romantic relationship review and it is very different from the romantic relationship history. You're now going to get very specific about the relationship you've chosen to work on first.

In the first review exercise, you'll put your memories about the relationship into graph form. In the second part of the review you'll convert the entries on the graph into short explanations of what happened and the emotions you had (and have) about them. In the third exercise you'll determine which of three completion categories you'll use to communicate what you've discovered that is unfinished for you.

You can complete your relationship only to what you're consciously aware of from your own memories. Do not use any methods or ideas that are not drawn strictly from things that you know for sure. Also, you can complete your relationship only with what is true for you. You must be careful to avoid doing this review by trying to figure out the other person's point of view. That would not be *your* truth. The more honest you can be about yourself, the more success you will have. Use this format exactly as suggested. It's always successful. Problems occur when people try to change the format. Please don't reinvent this wheel.

Warning—this is not something for couples to work on together. It's not appropriate to share what you're doing in this book with either your current or former partner.

The Graph—Creating an Accurate Reflection

The primary purpose of the graph part of the review is to help you create an accurate reflection of the relationship as you remember it. You're going to take a detailed look at the relationship, remembering specific events, both positive and negative. You'll put the positive events above the center line and the negative events below. No one else will have to see the graph, so you're free to be as honest as you would be in a journal or diary.

Although you may not realize it, this will *not* be the first time you've done a relationship review. You've been doing them all along. As relationships unfold, you constantly review what happens and all that has gone before. When you're happy and the relationship seems to be solid, those reviews are mostly positive. When things are going well you can talk about most problems with your mate and usually find ways to work them out. However, some of the problems just get pushed out of sight and come back into view only when the relationship starts to crumble. As things start going badly, the reviews become more painful. The balance of events seems more negative than positive. The disagreements and arguments become more frequent and last longer. At that point, a general sense of unhappiness often begins to dominate your feelings. And worse, any ability there might have been to talk about the problems and resolve them seems to diminish.

You may not have been aware that reviews like that were always going on, through good times and bad, except in the immediate aftermath of a battle. Those were the times when you went to your own instant replay machine and analyzed how he or she had been wrong, since you are "always right." It was in those reviews that you discovered things that you were not able to communicate to your partner or that you felt your partner never heard or understood. The problem was that you didn't know how to complete your discoveries. You only knew how to hold on to them and carry them forward.

Shopping List of Resentments

You may remember times when you felt as though your partner had dragged out what sounded like a shopping list of resentments and threw them in your face. We've yet to meet anyone who likes having someone else tell them about their flaws. We're sure that you didn't like it if that ever happened to you. On the other hand, it's likely that you've done the same. And as is true for many couples, you may have both stood there flinging shopping list items back and forth. For your part, after each argument, you probably added more to the shopping list of resentments that you carried around for later use.

The idea of the shopping list, coupled with the memories this review will bring to the surface, will help you realize that you've never known how to complete uncommunicated or unheard emotions. You may recognize that those shopping lists had become part of the emotional baggage you've been dragging with you. You may rediscover things that you've been reviewing and then burying as the relationship went into a tailspin.

You know them. You lived them. Even if you've pushed them away because they were too painful, they will come back as you do this exercise. You may also discover some things that you've never thought of before. Please let that be okay with you. What's not okay is if you shy away from them and leave them buried.

As you begin this exercise, write down everything that pops into your mind. After a while, you may discover many duplications where similar negative interactions happened over and over. They probably looked and sounded the same even though the arguments were on different topics. You don't need to list every battle you ever had. In fact, after you've listed three or four that are pretty much the same in terms of the feelings you had, you don't have to graph all the others. This also applies to positive events that you may not have communicated to your partner. After you've listed a few that seem essentially the same, you don't have to keep adding more.

Russell's Relationship Review

Before we throw you into the deep end, we will demonstrate Russell's review graph. After that, we'll give you instructions so you can get started. What appears in the figure is the relationship review Russell made of his relationship with his first wife, Vivienne. As you'll see, he put the positive events above the center line and the negative events below.

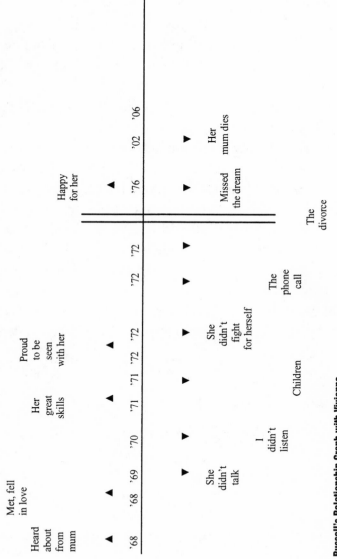

Russell's Relationship Graph with Vivienne

Last Exit before the Emotional Toll Booth

Having read Russell's relationship graph, you have a sense of what you will be doing next. But before you rush into it, we have some guidelines that will help ensure that you do your graph in a way that will give you the most benefit. At the end of the last chapter, we told you it was time to pick which relationship you are going to work on. If you haven't made that choice, make it now, so you can get to work.

Everything we've talked about and asked you to do so far has been in preparation for a larger set of actions. As you get ready to do your graph, you may realize that you're about to get into the real heart of the matter—your heart. For some of you, reviewing a relationship will be difficult. It will force you to accept the painful reality that the relationship is over. Even so, you must take this next set of actions or you will remain stuck in the old hopes and dreams and will not be able to create new ones. This is a point at which you might get scared and dig your heels in and refuse to move forward. Instead of freezing, we suggest that you acknowledge you're afraid and then take these new actions anyway. Honesty, courage, and willingness are all you have to bring to this exercise.

Focus on Yourself

As you begin, focus on your own actions and reactions rather than those of your partner. Be as honest as possible about the things you did and didn't do in the relationship. That will help you discover some truths about yourself that you couldn't see before. Taking responsibility for your reaction to what happened is the absolute key to completion. Be careful not to turn it into an indictment of your partner, so remember to graph the positive as well as negative things in the relationship.

Focusing on your part isn't that easy. Since it always seems easier to think about what the other person did, it requires more than a little discipline to look at yourself. As you reopen some of the areas that were difficult in the relationship, it may feel a little bit like tearing the scab off a wound. But if you don't do that and dig down and complete the unfinished business from the past, you're guaranteed to repeat your mistakes. Or even worse, you'll be so afraid of getting hurt again that you'll quit trying to find a relationship that fulfills your dreams.

Danger—Larger-than-Life Memory Pictures

It's not uncommon in the aftermath of a failed relationship to develop larger-than-life memory pictures. In those pictures, people tend to either bedevil or enshrine the other person. Neither is helpful in completing the unfinished emotions that are attached to the relationship that ended. Those kinds of exaggerated, one-sided memory pictures are really the function of a broken heart that doesn't know a better way to communicate the truth.

It's logical after a breakup to be more focused on the negative aspects of the relationship than on the positive. The positive ones are sometimes not easy to recall by the time a relationship ends. You might remember more positives at the beginning of the relationship. When you first fell in love you saw many wonderful qualities in the other person. Enter them on the graph regardless of how you feel now. You're going to review the relationship while taking responsibility for your part, including the things you said or did and your reaction to the things your partner said or did. This is where you have a chance to remember how you felt about all the events and interactions you recall, both positive and negative.

Begin at the Beginning

Your graph begins with your first conscious awareness of the person you became involved with. That was not necessarily the day the romance started. The beginning might not have been in person. It could have been by phone or letter or e-mail. Or as in Russell's relationship with Vivienne, when Viv's mum told him about her daughter, who was then in Paris. Nor does your emotional relationship end when the physical relationship ends or even after you've taken the actions to complete the relationship. In Russell's graph, he noted that he was affected when he found out Viv had had children and again when he learned that her mother had died.

Two Above and Two Below the Line

To maintain truth and accuracy, we strongly recommend that you have at least two positive, or above-the-line events, and at least two negative, or below-the-line events. You can have many events above or below the line, but the minimum of two in each area will help you avoid bedevilment or enshrinement. If you struggle with positives, just try to think of anything you liked about him or her. This could include how they looked, and it could also include sexual activities.

To avoid the danger of an inaccurate picture, you must be honest. While a partner may have been abusive at some levels, they may have paid the rent or provided food and clothing. We don't say this to minimize or justify bad behavior but to allow you to arrive at a truthful portrayal of the relationship. All relationships are made up of good and bad, right and wrong, sweet and sour, and sometimes ugly. Also, don't lose sight of the fact that you may have stayed long after you knew it was really over.

Unhappy or negative things can be as small as leaving the cap off the toothpaste or as large as infidelity and everything between. As with positive memories, none are too insignificant for this exercise. It's important to avoid comparing events and feelings and deciding that some aren't important enough to be on the graph. In fact, it is often the accumulation of small uncomfortable events that contribute to the failure of the relationship. Different kinds of events produce differing levels of emotional reactions. Use the length of your lines, above or below the horizontal, to indicate the intensity of your feelings at the time the event occurred. You get to be the judge. It doesn't matter whether there are more events above or below the line; it only matters that what's on the review is the truth. No one else gets a vote in your memories of your relationships.

Open Your Notebook and Begin

Open your notebook to a clean page and turn it sideways. Draw a line from left to right across the page. The left end of the line represents the beginning of the relationship. The beginning date is your first awareness of the other person. You may not remember the exact day, month, or year. That's okay. You don't need to have perfect details about dates. No matter when the relationship ended, the right end of the line represents the current year—enter it now. Next, add a vertical line and write in the year to indicate when the formal relationship ended. Make it a bold line so that it stands out to separate the end of the relationship from later events. If the relationship just ended, the end line and the bold line can be the same.

Keep in mind that relationships do not end entirely with the divorce or breakup. Russell's review noted events that happened years after the divorce. You may have some feelings about events that happened after the relationship was over. An obvious one could have been when you found out that your former mate was dating or in a relationship with someone new. Rarely does that kind of news fail to create emotions. That's the kind of event and reaction to add to your graph after the line that indicates the end of the relationship.

Now, go back to the beginning and reconstruct the relationship to the best of your ability. Let your memory wander. Mark down whatever pops into your mind. Decide if it is positive (above the line) or negative (below the line). You should vary the lengths of the lines to indicate the intensity you felt—the more intensity, the longer the line. Your mind may or may not go in chronological order. That's okay. Just identify positive and negative events. Make little notes on each of the events so you'll be able to remember what you meant. You may discover that there are many similar events that happened repeatedly, especially on the negative side. Put at least two or three of them down. You don't need more than a few of the same kinds of events to know that you were affected. As you do this, you might not think that every item you put down represents something incomplete. That's okay, but if it pops into your head, put it down anyway. Don't edit now, we'll do that later. Just recall and note. Honesty and thoroughness are essential.

This exercise may or may not be emotional for you. Just in case, have a box of tissues handy. Do not be preoccupied if you don't have much feeling when you do it. Everyone is different. What is most important is to be as honest as you can. If you get stuck, look back at Russell's example. It may trigger some memories for you. Our suggestion is to find a private place and set aside about an hour and then start.

When you finish the graph, you will have a choice to make. You can either put your notebook away or you can continue immediately with the second part of the relationship review.

CHAPTER NINE

CONVERTING THE GRAPH

Now it's time to convert your relationship graph into a series of short paragraphs that you'll use later to help you identify which aspects of the events you graphed remain emotionally incomplete. After Russell finished writing his graph, he wrote a short description of each event on the graph. To show you what it looks like, we've reprinted the story form of Russell's review here. In each dated story event, you'll notice that a sentence or phrase has been highlighted. They won't make sense to you just yet, but we'll explain them a little later.

Russell's Relationship Review in Story Form

*1968—We met on Sunday. We married on Tuesday. It may sound peculiar, but I already knew a good deal about Vivienne before I actually met her. Her mum and I worked together in a restaurant in Knightsbridge in London. Viv had been a student at the Sorbonne in Paris. In May of that year, the student riots erupted. Her mum was worried and encouraged her to come home. Viv returned to London on Saturday. We met on Sunday morning and went out on a date that night. I was smitten. I knew **she was the one for me**. Being from London, she seemed sophisticated to me. Looking back, I realize that, while she was only nineteen, her English accent and London ways made her seem older to me. As young as she was, I was only twenty-five.*

*1969—Our whirlwind courtship and marriage was accompanied by a major change, especially for Vivienne. We moved from the West End of London to West Hollywood, California. In addition to the culture shock for her, we were just getting to know each other. On some occasions she appeared to be upset with me, but she would never talk about it. My complaint was not that she was upset with me, but that she didn't communicate about it. She was very quiet but even more so when there was a problem. I often felt in the dark, and resorted to guessing what was going on with her. It was very frustrating. **I needed to forgive her for her unwillingness and inability to tell me what was going on**.*

1970—I am very verbal and can be self-righteous and dominating. I had some strong opinions about how we should run our business. Try as she might, she could not get me to budge on some self-defeating attitudes. She tried to reason with me, but most often I overruled her. Many decisions I made in those circumstances led to real business problems later. I have no doubt that they also contributed to our divorce. As I looked at my part of that relationship honestly, I realized that I owed her many apologies for my overbearing manner and inability to listen. I was sorry not just for what happened to me and the business, **but I needed to express how genuinely sorry I was that I had not been able to hear her as she tried to talk to me and help me.**

1971—We were very different people with different personalities and skills. When we opened our restaurant, our individual abilities created a nice combination. While I was the friendly host and kibitzer, she was exceptionally creative with cuisine and a magical baker. **Caught up in the business, I never took the opportunity to tell her how much I appreciated her skills and the wonderful balance she brought to the business aspect of our lives.**

1971—Personality issues aside, we didn't have too many major differences of opinions or philosophies. We were mostly in agreement about what we were doing and where we hoped it would lead. Except in one major area. She wanted children. It seemed very important to her. Having struggled so much of my early life, and finally feeling some freedom, I was not at all ready to have children. Viv didn't seem to understand. I **needed to forgive her for any part the issue of children played in her asking for the divorce. I also needed to apologize for not having recognized and told the truth about myself sooner.**

*1972—During our four years together, there was tremendous joy. We entertained and were entertained by celebrities. We were the toast of the town. It was exciting to be with her at many events. Being caught in the energy of our lifestyle and our business, I did not always remember to stop and put into words the important emotions I was experiencing. While we said the obligatory "I love you" every night, **I needed to tell her how much she'd meant to me, how proud I was to be seen with her, and how wonderful I thought she was.***

*1972—I was usually preoccupied with the daily goings-on in our restaurant. I was not as conscious of what was going on in our marriage. **I have already said that I owed her some apologies for my overbearing ways.** It would be unrealistic to look at this relationship and conclude that it was only my part or my flaws that destroyed it. While I needed to apologize for my self-righteous verbal dominance, **I also needed to forgive her for her quietness and unwillingness to fight for what she believed in. I needed to forgive her for giving up and giving in.***

*1972—As the marriage progressed, there was great confusion for me. On the one hand, I was blissfully happy and unaware that there was trouble in paradise. We had a successful business and to the best of my limited awareness, a happy marriage. On the other hand, those problem areas that I can now see with much clarity were building up a head of steam. One day, Vivienne called me and announced that she was leaving me and applying for a divorce. That telephone call sticks out in my memory. She did not try to talk to me in person but did it on the phone. **For me it was another exam-***

*ple of how she did not communicate, and I needed to for-
give her for doing it that way.*

*1972—For me, the divorce was very sudden. I don't know
how I am alive, because I can't imagine how I drove a car in
the first several weeks following the divorce. I must have
walked and talked, but I remember almost nothing. My only
conscious awareness about dealing with loss was to be strong
for others. Now I was the other, and I didn't know what to do.
During that time, I had a revelation. It dawned on me that
my biggest complaint was that when there was a problem she
wouldn't talk. On the other hand, I realized that when she
did talk I didn't listen. I didn't know what to do with this
awareness.* **It was much later that I realized that I needed
to forgive her for not talking about her feelings and to
apologize to her for not listening when she did talk.**

(Note: The divorce ended the marital relationship
and ended the day-to-day physical connection. But
some aspects of the emotional and spiritual relationship
continued. In the more than thirty years since the
divorce, Russell reports that there have been a few
notable events that provoked emotions for him. The
next two entries show what we mean.)

*1976—I heard from Vivienne that she and her new hus-
band had adopted two baby boys and shortly thereafter she
had become pregnant and delivered a baby girl. My reaction
at the time was very mixed. Of course I was thrilled for her.
I had always believed she would be a fabulous mother, but a
part of me was hurt. A part of me flashed back to some old
hopes, dreams, and expectations that I had had when we*

were together. **I was reminded of the sadness I had that the dream of having children with her had not come true.**

2002—I received a note from Vivienne, who now lives in Spain. Her mum had died. Viv sent along a copy of the obituary notice from the London Times. *The note brought with it a host of memories and feelings. Having long ago done what I'd needed to do to become emotionally complete,* **I could react to the sad news and talk openly about my former relationships with Viv and with her mother.**

Different, Better, More— Hopes, Dreams, Expectations

There are those six words again. We've used them several times before and we repeated them here on purpose. We want the ideas contained in those words to help guide you as you do this review. You're now going to take an in-depth look at a relationship with an eye to discovering the things you wish had been *different* or *better* or there had been *more* of and the unrealized *hopes*, *dreams*, and *expectations* you had about the future. You'll be looking for the things you wish you'd said or not said. You'll be looking for the things you wish you'd done or not done. And you'll be looking for the same kinds of things you wish the other person had said or done or not said or done. You'll find those things in both the positive and negative events you remember and put on your graph.

You may have done a lot of soul-searching in the aftermath of a relationship. You may have done a lot of "work" trying to understand what happened and why. You may have done therapy or twelve-step programs, or followed any number of spiritual paths trying to rebuild yourself. We know a lot of people who've done some or all of those things and received great benefit from them all. Sometimes having done so much of that kind of work creates the illusion that there's nothing left to learn or do. We've had people tell us that they have no regrets about a relationship that ended. Yet they showed up at our doorstep looking for help. Having no regrets is wonderful but it doesn't equal emotional completion. We've also had people tell us, "I told him everything—there's not one thing I didn't say." And they too showed up at our door. Telling everything to someone usually doesn't create completion; in fact, it often creates the opposite, as you'll see a little later when we talk about completion categories.

No matter how much work people have done, we've yet to meet anyone who arrived at our door without undelivered emotional communications about the relationships that had ended. As you move forward, we want you to understand that this review and the completion of unfinished emotional business does not interfere with any therapy-based actions you've taken or spiritual beliefs you may have. Don't let the work you've done in the past stop you from doing this exercise and the ones that follow. Let us suggest that we honor the work you've done before getting to this book as having helped you discover that there's something that still needs to be completed. You cannot hurt anyone or anything by doing this; you can only gain.

Writing Your Short Explanations

Russell wrote a short paragraph to explain each of the entries on his review graph. In doing that, he was able to translate the events he had recalled into story form so they made sense and so he could later recognize what was emotionally incomplete for each entry. You're about to do the same thing. We hope you now have a general sense of how to write out your stories. Here are some specific instructions:

- Set aside about an hour, with the ever-present box of tissues, just in case.
- Get out your notebook.
- Turn to the page on which you wrote out your relationship review graph. Look at the first event you plotted. Turn to a clean page in your notebook and write down the year the event happened (approximate if necessary) and then write a short paragraph about it.
- **After each entry, leave at least two blank lines. You will come back and add something in those spaces in the next exercise**.
- Go back to the graph and pick up the next event and follow the same procedure for each event on your graph.

- Imagine that you were allowed a few sentences to tell someone about each event—what happened and how you felt about it—either positive or negative.
- Take your time with this part of the exercise. Think about each of the events before you write them out. Again, keep in mind that no one else will see or read this, so be as bone-honest as you can.

Go write your stories now.

When you're done, take a little break. Let what you've graphed and written sink in. You can continue right to the next exercise or you can take a few hours or even a day or two off before moving to the next and last part of this exercise. If you take a break, remember to put your notebook in a safe and private place.

CHAPTER TEN

THREE CATEGORIES THAT CONVEY EVERYTHING IMPORTANT

There are three completion categories that will help you convey anything that is emotionally incomplete between you and the person in the relationship you've been working on.

forgiveness
apologies
significant emotional statements

These categories may seem simple, but they will need some explanation. As we clarify them, we will explain those highlighted comments in Russell's review stories.

At the end of each of his stories there is a phrase that represents an undelivered emotional communication. You may have noticed them, but you may not have realized that each of those highlighted comments fell into one of the three completion categories—forgiveness, apologies, or significant emotional statements. You also may not have realized that Russell didn't actually issue the forgiveness or apologies. He simply said that he needed to. Here's one that illustrates the idea: *For me it was another example of how she did not communicate, and I needed to forgive her for doing it that way.*

As Russell wrote out his graph and then the short stories, he discovered many emotional communications that had been left unfinished at the end of his relationship with Vivienne. The next action was for him to convert them into one or more of the three completion categories. We are now going to spend some time explaining the three categories so you'll be prepared for the next step of converting what is emotionally unfinished for you.

But I Can't Forgive

The inability or unwillingness to forgive is one of the most common resistances we hear. Relationships end because people are unable to live out the commitments and promises they made to each other. Therefore there are always things that each person needs to forgive. Along the way, some pretty harsh things often get said and done. Although forgiveness is very helpful, it's a difficult topic at best, and it becomes even harder when we are reeling from the emotional hurt that follows a breakup. Before you even think about forgiving, we want you to read this next section very carefully.

Forgiveness Is Giving Up the Hope of a Different or Better Yesterday

Nonforgiveness is a demand that can never be met. What it means is that you want the world to turn backward to the event that caused your pain so it can come out differently. The saddest part of nonforgiveness is that the nonforgiving person is the one who continues to suffer.

That idea of giving up an impossible demand engages a new understanding of what forgiveness really is and suggests how helpful it can be when used properly. It shows just how stuck you can become in the past, which automatically restricts your future. Forgiveness is still one of the least understood concepts in the world. Most people seem to convert the word *forgive* into the word *condone*. We don't know exactly how this confusion evolved, but the definitions in *Merriam-Webster's Tenth Collegiate Dictionary* help illustrate the problem.

Forgive: "to cease to feel resentment against (an offender)."

Condone: "to treat as if trivial, harmless, or of no importance."

If you simply use the dictionary definition of forgive, you're on the right track. However, if you believe that *forgive* and *condone* are synonymous, it's virtually impossible to ever forgive. The implication that you might trivialize a horrible event is clearly unacceptable. Any resentment of past events limits and restricts your ability to participate fully in life. Any reminder of the person or the event may stimulate a painful reliving of the unfinished emotions attached to it. Successful recovery requires completion of the pain rather than retention of the resentment. You are the only one who suffers when you don't forgive.

The subject of forgiveness carries with it many beliefs, passed from generation to generation. Most of those beliefs do not reflect the simple and accurate definition in the dictionary. Some people have developed such a massive resistance to the word *forgive* that they cannot use it. We recently helped such a woman. She called it the F word. We gave her the following phrase to use in place of forgive: *I acknowledge the things that you did or did not do that hurt me, and I'm not going to let them hurt me anymore.* A variation of phrase is to say, *I acknowledge the things that you did or did not do that hurt me, and I'm not going to let my memory of those incidents hurt me anymore.*

Forgiveness Is an Action, Not a Feeling

Many people say, "I can't forgive him; I don't feel it." To which we say, "Of course not, you cannot feel something you haven't done." You cannot feel forgiveness until you do it. What's more, in all likelihood you'll never "feel" like forgiving someone who has harmed you. You will have to force yourself to take the action of forgiveness, and to do that you have to understand that you are the real beneficiary of the forgiveness. It's what lets you out of your emotional prison. A feeling of forgiveness can only result from the action of verbalizing the forgiveness. *Action first, feeling follows.* However, the forgiveness must never be spoken directly to the person who is being forgiven. We'll explain that in just a little bit.

Forgiveness is the result of giving up the resentment you hold against another person. You may need to forgive them for something they actually did ("I forgive you for lying to me") or for something they did not do ("I forgive you for not helping with the children"). You may need to forgive them for a tone of voice you perceived to be dismissive. It doesn't matter whether they intended it to sound that way. What matters is what you believed and how it affected you emotionally.

There's another strange expression: "I can forgive, but I can't forget." It mixes two separate ideas that are not directly connected. Imagine that your mate had called you stupid every day for years. It's not even vaguely possible to forget those incidents. The implication of "I can forgive, but I can't forget" is that since I cannot forget, I will not forgive. But ask yourself, Who stays in jail? Who continues to resent and, in so doing, shuts down their own mind, body, and heart? Whose life is limited by the lack of forgiveness?

As we mentioned, forgiveness must always be communicated indirectly. That's not an arbitrary statement. The reason for that is because forgiveness is always perceived as an attack. When you forgive someone, in effect, you are telling them that you are right and they are wrong. No one will sit still for you to tell them they're wrong. You wouldn't either. You will automatically defend yourself anytime you feel attacked.

We're often asked whether it's ever appropriate to forgive someone directly, in person, or in any other way where they would know they are being forgiven. Our response is *No! No! No!* The person being forgiven need never know that it has happened. ***Remember, never forgive anyone directly to their face. Or on the phone, or in a letter, or an e-mail.*** Those are just variations on direct communication.

Many people ask others to forgive them. We think this is a very incorrect communication. In fact, when you ask for forgiveness, you are being manipulative: you are asking the other person to do something that you need to do. When you ask for forgiveness, you're really trying to apologize for something you've said or done.

In that case it's clear that *you* need to take an action, not ask someone else to do it for you.

I need to forgive you so I can be free.

When people struggle with forgiveness, we suggest that they add the simple phrase, *so I can be free*, which helps them remember just who they are trying to help when they forgive. It may be true that the insensitive, unconscious, and sometimes evil actions of our former mates may have hurt us. But it is *our* continued resentment and lack of forgiveness that hurts us, not them. Imagine that the person who harmed you has died. Can your continued resentment harm him or her? Clearly not! Can it harm you? Unfortunately, yes. When we use any of the completion categories, our objective is to set ourselves free. We forgive to reacquire our own sense of well-being.

Forgiveness has nothing to do with the other person.

Forgiveness is only for you—use it to set yourself free.

Apologies

Apologies can be difficult too. As with forgiveness, the absence of an accurate definition contributes to the problem. Let's start by defining *apology* for the purposes of the work we're doing. A definition for *apology* in our *Merriam-Webster* best explains what we mean: "an admission of error or discourtesy accompanied by an

expression of regret." We add to that definition by saying that you need to apologize for anything that you did
or did not do that may have hurt your partner. You may
owe an apology for something you actually did ("I'm
sorry that I lied to you") or for something you did not
do ("I'm sorry I wasn't more helpful with the children"). As you can see, these are the flip side of the forgiveness we demonstrated, which shows that each
partner can view the same event from a different perspective. But you get to communicate about only what
you did or did not do or your reaction to what your
partner did or did not do. There are times when you
will have to communicate in two categories. For example, "I forgive you for being so abrupt and ordering me
around" and "I'm sorry that I was so reactive and took
it out on you in many ways."

So far we've asked you to focus on the things you
actually said or did that might have hurt your partner.
But you cannot overlook the negative thoughts and
judgments you had about them even though you may
never have said them. You still need to apologize, *indirectly*, for those thoughts. As with most apologies, those
that relate to your private thoughts should and must
remain indirect. Occasionally you will discover some
apologies that can safely be made to your former mate
when and if the situation permits. However, the circumstances that surround most romantic endings do
not encourage or support that kind of interaction. For
a variety of reasons, including the fact that your ex has

not necessarily been taking actions to become emotionally complete, most attempts to communicate directly about such matters fail. Even if he or she was doing what you're doing in this book, his or her perception of what happened and who was at fault will be different from yours.

Victim Mentality Makes Apologies Difficult

In reaction to awkward, difficult, or abusive events, some people develop lifelong relationships to those events. As a result, they often adopt what might be called a victim mentality. From that position, they find it difficult to believe that they ever have to apologize, since they always feel as if they have been wronged. They have a hard time taking responsibility for the things that they've done or said that might have harmed others. Within a relationship, they will often perceive themselves as victim of their mates. Unfortunately, that's a familiar position based on past and not necessarily current reality. It places a burden on the mate who must be on constant alert to never say or do anything that could be perceived as hurtful. Later, we'll give you some guidance about completing other kinds of relationships that may have caused you to perceive yourself as a victim.

You cannot become complete with anything less than the whole truth. From time to time in all relationships, each partner can and will feel hurt by the other. Even if you feel your partner offended more than you did, you must apologize for your part. There's a need to apologize for your transgressions, no matter how slight, no matter how infrequent. To repeat, most of the apologies should be made in the context of this work and not made directly to your former partner.

Right or Complete—Pick One

Sometimes our need to be right can be a big problem in making apologies. Our sense of rightness or self-righteousness can keep us from being totally honest about our actions and nonactions. Because relationship endings tend to be filled with our own one-sided analysis of who was right and who was wrong, we must be especially alert in the area of apologies. There's a tendency to get caught up in the idea that since the other person has harmed you, you don't have to apologize. While it's true that you feel hurt by what they did, that doesn't eliminate your need to apologize for the things you had done to them.

Significant Emotional Statements

The third major category for communicating undelivered emotional thoughts and feelings is called significant emotional statements. Any communication that is important to you and is neither a forgiveness nor an apology will conveniently fall into this catchall category.

Here are a few examples:

Positive	Negative
Thanks for being so wonderful with my family.	I hated every time you made plans for us without consulting me.
I appreciated your support when I was out of work.	I hated it when you embarrassed me in public.
Thanks for leaving the frosting for me—my favorite part.	I was so hurt that you never said, "I love you," unless I asked you to.
Thanks for taking care of me when I was ill.	It was so hard to talk to you; I felt I had to walk on eggshells.

The significant emotional statement category is both simple and profound. It allows you to say anything that is keeping you incomplete. Although the individual statements might appear to be minor, **it is the accumulation of undelivered emotional communications that build up in a relationship that contributes to a sense of incompleteness.** You definitely don't want to carry that accumulation into your next relationship. There may be things that you said to your partner that you don't believe they ever really heard. Saying them again in this context can be helpful.

Important alert: All negative significant emotional statements must be accompanied by forgiveness. Using an example from the preceding ones, here's how you do that: "I hated every time you made plans for us without consulting me." **I need to forgive you for each time you did that**. If you fail to issue the forgiveness for anything negative, you will not achieve completion. To understand what we mean, think about anyone you know who has been repeating a painful negative story about how someone harmed them. What you may now realize is that since there is no forgiveness attached there is no completion, just an endless loop.

Identifying What Is Incomplete for You

We have repeated the idea that when relationships end there are always things we wish had been *different* or *better* or there had been *more* of to help you understand what incompleteness really is. In effect, it was under the heading of those three words that you found the things that make you incomplete with your former mate. When you created your romantic relationship review you were actually using those ideas to make your discoveries. In simple terms, the negative things you put below the line are things you wish had been *different* or *better*. The positive things that you put above the line are the ones you wish you'd had *more* of or had communicated about.

When a relationship ends, there are always broken *hopes*, *dreams*, and *expectations*. Although by the time we arrive at a divorce or breakup, those hopes and dreams may seem long ago and far away. Nevertheless, those feelings that were attached to the early part of the relationship are a major aspect of the unfinished emotions that must be communicated as significant emotional statements. Now is the time to put words on the thoughts and feelings that the ending robbed you of the opportunity to communicate. The significant emotional statement category gives you the opportunity to communicate about the hopes and dreams that are not going to come true.

Gratitude Is Emotionally Significant

In our search for truth within relationships that have ended, we must not overlook the things for which we are grateful to our partner. Even though the roughness of the ending often obscures better times, we need to communicate the positive things we feel or felt at some point. There are probably some things for you that fall under the heading of gratitude. There are several examples in the short list we made to demonstrate significant emotional statements. The first one was "Thanks for being so wonderful with my family." It could also be stated as an apology: "I'm sorry I never told you how much I appreciated the way you were with my family. Thank you." In that case, the apology is followed by the simple, significant statement "Thank you."

Never Deliver Negative Statements Directly

In dealing with living people, it's never appropriate to make a negative significant emotional statement directly to them. We use the same guidelines for this category as we do in dealing with forgiveness. Since completion is your ultimate goal, you must be aware of what you do that supports completion or undermines it.

We hope you now have a clearer understanding of what we mean when we use the categories forgiveness, apologies, and significant emotional statements. We know that the way we teach forgiveness is very different from most other schools of thought. We are also aware that our idea about not confronting anyone with forgiveness or any negative significant comments is not universally understood or applied. The objective of what we teach is completion of unfinished emotional business. If you attack or confront someone, even if you believe what you're saying is true, it will create more unfinished business, not completion. You cannot make the assumption that the person you are forgiving agrees with you. In fact, it is unlikely to be so.

Adding Recovery Categories to Your Story Entries

Now it's time for you to add the recovery categories to each of your short stories. First, look back at Russell's review stories in the beginning of chapter 9. In his comments about each of the incidents on his review, you'll notice that an undelivered emotional communication is highlighted. As we mentioned a little earlier, those comments are phrased in a certain way. Russell says, "**I need to forgive you**," and "**I need to apologize**." He doesn't actually issue the forgiveness or apology at that time.

As you read over Russell's review again, it will help you understand how to identify the undelivered emotional communication in each of your story lines. Since there are only the three categories, you shouldn't have much trouble deciding if you need to forgive, apologize, or make a significant statement. Keep in mind that some of your stories will require communication in more than one category. For example, one of Russell's is "It was much later that I realized that I needed to forgive her for not talking about her feelings and to apologize to her for not listening when she did talk."

You may have strong feelings about many of the things that happened in the relationship. It's okay to be angry, sad, frustrated, confused, or anything else you feel. Don't judge yourself for having feelings. Don't fall into the trap of analyzing or intellectualizing everything you've remembered. We want you to look for the feelings you had when these events happened and some of the ones you may have carried forward. Stay focused on the relationship you're working on, though other people and relationships may pop into your mind.

Set aside an hour and have a box of tissues, just in case. Now get out your notebook and go to your romantic relationship review. You can use both the graph and the stories to help you. You're going to go through them one event at a time and assign a completion category to everything you've put in your stories. This is why we told you, **after each entry, leave at least two blank lines. You will come back and add something in those spaces in the next exercise.** You're going to enter your completion category comments in those spaces now. When you've done that, the relevant forgiveness, apologies, or significant emotional statements that you need to make will be attached to each of your stories.

You may not feel incomplete about some of your entries, but convert them into the categories anyway. You can't lose anything by doing that. Generally speaking, above-the-line events will be either apologies or significant emotional statements. In Russell's romantic relationship review with his former wife, Viv, he said, "Caught up in the business, I never took the opportunity to tell her how much I appreciated her skills and the wonderful balance she brought to the business aspect of our lives." When he converted that into a category, it became a need to issue an apology. He wrote, "Viv, I need to apologize that I never told you how much I appreciated your skills and about the positive things that you contributed to our business. Thank you." You notice that at the end, he adds, "Thank you," which becomes a significant emotional statement.

Below-the-line events will require forgiveness or significant emotional statements. Some events may require both categories, *especially negative events*. In another part of Russell's review he says, "Viv didn't seem to understand. I needed to forgive her for any part the issue of children played in her asking for the divorce." That was converted into two categories. The first half is a significant emotional statement, and the second half contains the forgiveness. He wrote, "Viv, it saddens me that you didn't understand that I wasn't ready to have children. I need to forgive you for not being willing to wait for me."

It's not uncommon for some events to have both positive and negative elements. For example, perhaps your mate bought you a gym membership as a gift and then kept nagging you to go work out. Your completion communication for that would be, "Thank you for buying me the gym membership, and I forgive you for nagging me to go."

When you began the review graph, we suggested that if you found similar events that happened repeatedly, you could list a few, but you didn't need to recite each and every one. Now, as you convert the events into the emotional categories, you can consolidate them even further. The key is to distill them so that your comments mainly represent undelivered emotional communications. After you've weeded out the repetitive events, you should have an entry for those that remain in at least one completion category. Don't be overly concerned if you repeat communications that you think you've already said directly to your partner. It's perfectly okay to restate any forgivenesses, apologies, or significant emotional statements that you made in the past. Also, don't worry if you've listed more than one event that needs the same completion communication. Shortly, you'll have an opportunity to refine everything that you've done in this exercise.

Start the work. When you finish, put your notebook in a safe and private place.

MOVING TO COMPLETION

You're now ready to complete what you've discovered that is unfinished for you in the relationship. Since the relationship ended, or shifted from positive to negative, you've probably become familiar with the pain you associate with it. Now's the time to complete your relationship with that pain by effectively delivering what was unfinished for you so you can move forward in your life.

A Farewell Letter Isn't a Completion Letter

At the suggestion of well-meaning friends or professionals, many people write farewell letters to their former romantic partners. It's possible that you've written one of those letters. Although it didn't hurt you, it left you looking for more help, which brought you to this book. If you wonder why, it's because a farewell letter, without proper content, usually only creates a measure of short-term relief but lacks long-term benefit. All too often, farewell letters are merely a recitation of events and emotions, much like a newsletter. Most such attempts at completion are unsuccessful. To be successful, it's essential that the content of the letter is communicated in completion categories rather than in the style of an emotional newsletter. That's why we spent so much time explaining the three categories so you can convert the work you've done into a **completion letter**.

The Relationship Completion Letter

Writing the letter will help you become emotionally complete with everything about the relationship that has been unfinished for you until now. You will now be able to say good-bye to what is emotionally incomplete for you. You will be able to say good-bye to any pain you associate with the relationship, including all of the unmet hopes, dreams, and expectations. You can say good-bye to the unrealistic expectation of getting something from someone who could not or would not give it. While you will become complete with anything painful, you will be able to keep any fond memories of the relationship. And at last, you will be able to move on.

Some of you may never see or hear from your former partner again. Others of you will maintain a friendship or connection because you have children or just because you wish to. For those of you who are obliged to have contact but do not really relish that idea, this letter will help you deal with that awkward situation. Keep in mind that the forgiveness aspects of this letter will help create emotional freedom for you. What is most important is that you finally attain the freedom to restart your life so that you can find happiness in a long-term loving relationship.

Relationship Completion Letter Example

Here's a shortened version of Russell's completion letter to Viv. It contains enough examples to help you see how to construct your letter, but we'll also give you detailed instructions.

Dear Viv,

I have been reviewing our relationship and have discovered some things I want to say.

Viv, I forgive you for not telling me what was going on with you.

Viv, It saddens me that you didn't understand that I wasn't ready to have children. I forgive you for not being willing to wait for me.

Viv, I forgive you for how you ended the relationship.

Viv, I apologize for being overbearing.

Viv, I apologize for not listening to you and for not hearing what you were trying to tell me.

Viv, I apologize that I never told you how much I appreciated your skills and about the positive things that you contributed to our business. Thank you.

Viv, I want you to know how proud I was to be seen with you.

Viv, I want you to know that I am positive that you are a fabulous mother. And from time to time, I have been sad that you and I did not get to be parents together.

Viv, I have to go now,

Goodbye, Viv.

Instructions for Your Completion Letter

Writing the letter is best done alone and in one complete session. Writing the letter can be an emotionally painful experience, and there's too much temptation to avoid the pain. You've already proven your courage; use it now to write this letter. Many people have known for a long time what wasn't emotionally complete; they just didn't know what to do about it. You know what you have to do; now you need to do it.

Specific instructions: Allow at least an hour. The most effective way to write your letter is to have your romantic relationship review and your lists of forgiveness, apologies, and significant emotional statements in front of you. Look over the review and the lists and then write your letter. Although your review and lists may contain many repetitions, it's not necessary to repeat the same completion communications over and over. Use this letter to consolidate them into the most concise expression possible. Your letter should be primarily focused on the completion categories.

There's no limit on how much you can write, but the emotional intensity is often lost in volume. This is your opportunity to say the most important unsaid things as well as those things you feel your partner never really heard. There may be things that you remember saying and you believe your partner heard but you still feel a need to say again in this letter. Please do. Generally, two or three standard pages is sufficient. It's okay to write a little more or a little less. If you have more than five pages, you probably need to look to see if you are repeating the same things.

Writing the letter may or may not be an emotional experience for you. Don't be preoccupied if it's not emotional. We're each different and unique. Just be as honest as you possibly can. Keep in mind that the letter will never be seen or heard by the person it is written to. Because it contains forgiveness and negative statements, it's not safe or appropriate for them to read or hear. The fact that they'll never see it gives you safety to be totally honest.

In spite of the hurtful—and sometimes abusive— things that happen in relationships, some people get to this point and have a sense of compassion for their former mates. They want to say, "You did the best you could with what you had to work with." While that sounds okay, it really isn't. It inadvertently excuses or defends bad behavior and negates the forgivenesses you are issuing in the letter. Perhaps you're aware that your mate had been mistreated in childhood. Even if that's true, it doesn't make it okay that they hurt you in any way. Since you've followed our suggestions, you'll be forgiving them for anything they did that harmed you. Having done that, if you do feel some compassion for them, the best way to say it is, "I want you to know that I have compassion for you and the things you've had to deal with in your life." As you can see that statement does not excuse or condone anything they may have done to you. This comment should be made at the end of the significant emotional statement category.

It's time for you to begin. Here is a helpful format for your letter.

Dear Fred,
    I have been reviewing our relationship, and I discovered some things that I want to tell you.
    Fred, I forgive you for . . .

Fred, I forgive you for . . .

Fred, I forgive you for . . .

Fred, I apologize for . . .

Fred, I apologize for . . .

Fred, I apologize for . . .

Fred, I want you to know . . . [significant emotional statement]

Fred, I want you to know . . . [significant emotional statement]

Fred, I want you to know . . . [significant emotional statement]

(You may have more than three entries in each category. Most people find it helpful to keep them grouped in categories, but that's just a suggestion.)

Closing Your Letter

To complete what you've discovered, you must end your letter effectively. When you speak to a friend on the phone, you conclude the conversation with the word *good-bye* to signal the end of that conversation. We conclude our completion letter with "good-bye" to signal the end of this communication.

Other kinds of completion letters usually end with expressions of love or fond regards, but that is not normally the case after romantic relationships have ended. The most effective and accurate closing is simply, "I have to go now, and I have to let go of the pain. Good-bye,

Fred." However, some people choose to end their letter with, "I love you, I miss you. Good-bye, Fred."

You can create other closing statements based on what is truthful for you. What should remain constant are the very last words, "Good-bye, Fred." Failure to say good-bye can often negate all the good work you've done. **It is the *good-bye* that completes the communication**. Please don't substitute other words. Not saying good-bye leaves the communication open and runs the risk of leaving you incomplete.

As we said, allow at least an hour. Have a box of tissues handy, just in case.

When you finish, put your completion letter in a safe and private place.

CHAPTER

TWELVE

IF A TREE FALLS IN THE FOREST . . .

Our workshops are attended by people who are dealing with a death or a divorce or other major loss issues. One woman once arrived at a workshop five years after the death of her husband. She gave up three full days of her life and a substantial amount of dollars to attend along with twelve other people. From the first morning of the workshop, she maintained that she'd already done the work about her husband who had died. We didn't argue with her, we just said okay. We figured that if she was willing to give up three days to attend a seminar, she must have left something out. The Personal Workshops we did in those days used a variation of the exercises we use in our Relationship Seminars today and that you have done in this book.

Indeed, she had already done everything we have asked you to do and done it pretty much the same way we suggest. At every juncture along the way she said, "I did that," and then we said, "Okay, do it again." We knew there would have to come a moment when she would say, "Uh-oh, there it is, that's what I didn't do." She'd written a letter, very much like the one you've just written. She managed to have the comments she made in the three categories we've spelled out for you, because that's the most logical way to say those kinds of things. She'd even taken the letter out to her husband's grave and read it out loud. And she still wound up at our workshop years later.

What was missing? Have you figured it out yet?

In the workshop, at a point exactly parallel to where you are now, we announced, "**Undelivered communications of an emotional nature must be verbalized**," and "**They must be heard by another living human being to be effective**."

There was a gasp in the room. It was her. She had found the missing piece of her puzzle. Even though she had read the letter, out loud, at the grave, it had not been heard by another living person. Of course there were some new elements in the letter she wrote this time, as many things had occurred in her life since he died. But the basic forgiveness, apologies, and significant emotional statements were not radically different.

Our brains can be somewhat stubborn. No matter what our spiritual or religious beliefs may be, the unconscious mind demands a living observer to attest to the completeness of our communication. We're not trying to be mystical or psychologically technical; it's merely that our practical experience in helping people become emotionally complete has taught us what works and what doesn't. At this point, we believe that you are 98 percent emotionally complete in your relationship with the person about whom you wrote the relationship review and the completion letter. The last 2 percent is your new 100 percent. You must read the letter out loud to a living human being so it can become a completed communication for you. Here are some very specific guidelines for reading your letter, both for you and for the listener.

Choosing Your Listener

The person who listens to you read your letter *cannot* be the person to whom it is written.

The person who listens to you read your letter *cannot* be the person to whom it is written.

The person who listens to you read your letter *cannot* be the person to whom it is written.

Are we perfectly clear that you cannot read the letter to your former partner?

Now just in case you haven't figured out, there is another someone who is *not* an appropriate listener.

That's right, if you have a *current partner*, he or she *cannot* be your listener.

There are many other people who cannot be the audience for your letter, including your former partner's brother, sister, mother, father, friend, or pretty much anyone who has or had a relationship with him or her. Most of your own friends also had a relationship with your partner, so they bring their own feelings, good, bad, or mixed, and are not good choices to listen to your letter. You don't want to put anyone in an awkward situation as the result of hearing what you've written in your letter. Since you're telling your version of the truth with your emotions attached, your listener will need to be as close to neutral as possible about the other person.

You may have contacts with people from areas of your life who did not know your mate. They might make better candidates. A therapist, clergyperson, or another, who already has an understanding of the need to have the highest level of confidentiality, is also a good choice. The listener must commit, in advance, to absolute confidentiality. They must agree that they will never tell anyone what they heard when you read your letter. If they are unwilling to make that commitment, find someone else. Next you will ask them to read the "Instructions for the Listener" that follow. They must agree to each of the seven following guidelines. No compromises! No exceptions!

Instructions for the Listener

1. Your first instruction is to adopt the image of a **heart with ears**. It is your job to listen and listen only. You may laugh or cry if appropriate, but *you must not talk at all*. Nothing about what you do can imply judgment, criticism, or analysis.

2. Take a position at least a few feet away from the reader. We don't want you in the reader's face; it can be a little intimidating. Let your body be relaxed. You are listening to an important personal communication. Do not have pen or paper in your hands or lap. Take off your watch, so that you don't inadvertently glance at it.

3. During the letter reading, do not touch the reader at all. At this juncture, touch usually stops feelings. Although not everyone is emotional when reading, we do not want to inhibit feelings if they happen. The reader will have his or her own tissues handy.

4. There's a very real possibility that you will be affected by listening to what is read. Please let that be okay with you. However, you must keep in mind that this is not about you. So, to a limited degree, you have to control the intensity of your reaction. On the other hand, if tears well up in your eyes, please leave them there. If you wipe them away, you give the message that tears are bad.

5. Your presence is important to the reader. You must stay *in the moment*, even though your head or your heart may want to pull you away. Listen with your heart on behalf of the reader.

6. As soon as the reader says good-bye, immediately offer a hug. You will have a sense of how long the hug should last. Don't rush it. The letter has been a culmination of some very demanding work.

7. Do not analyze, judge, or criticize. It's not necessarily a good idea to talk about the experience afterward. Talking tends to lead to analysis, judgment, or intellectualizing.

Instructions for the Letter Reader

1. Choose a place that is totally safe for you. Avoid public places.

2. Bring along a box of tissues. Keep the tissues where you can get them if you need them. We don't want your listener handing them to you.

3. Before you start reading your letter, close your eyes. Although you have enlisted the help of a listener, your objective is to read the letter to whom it was written. Get a mental image of the person you are completing with if you can. (We don't recommend using photographs as they lock you into a specific time and place.)

4. Open your eyes. Start reading your letter. You may or may not have an emotional response to your reading. Either way is okay. If you start to choke up, try to talk while you cry. The emotions are contained in the words you have written. Try to push the words up and out of your mouth. Do not swallow your words or your feelings.

5. When you get to the very end, before reading your good-bye sentence, close your eyes, get an image of the person again, and say your final words. This may be accompanied by many tears. If so, make sure you get the words spoken, *especially the good-bye.*

Remember, you're saying good-bye to the pain and you're saying good-bye to any unfinished business. You're *not* saying good-bye to the fond memories. Say good-bye to the emotional incompleteness. Say good-bye to the pain, isolation, and confusion. Say good-bye to the physical relationship that you had but has now ended. Say good-bye and then let it be okay that you cry and let it all out. Also, let it be okay if you don't cry. It's essential that you say good-bye, or the relationship probably will remain incomplete for you.

6. As soon as you finish, ask your listener for a hug. You might want and need the hug to be quite long. Don't cut it short. You may find yourself sobbing for a while. Let that be okay with you. You've probably been holding on to the pain for a while. Don't rush the feelings.

What to Do with the Letter

People ask us what they should do with their completion letter after they've read it out loud to someone they
trust. We can't really tell you what to do. It's a very personal decision. We do caution you that if you keep your
letter, keep it in a very secure place. The last thing you
want is for someone to find it. This is especially important if you have children and you wrote the letter about
their other parent.

The Afterglow or the Aftermath

We cannot predict how you will feel after reading your
letter. The range of possible emotions is as wide and
deep as the diversity of individual personalities. Some
people feel an instant sense of freedom and like a
thousand-pound weight was released. Others feel
heavy and sad. Still others feel nothing at all or even
numb. What we know to be true is that whatever you
feel is normal and natural and will be a reflection of
how you react to your own emotions or absence of
them. Please let whatever you do or don't feel be okay
with you.

   The reason we gave such firm instructions for both
the listener and the reader about not analyzing after the
reading is precisely because whatever you feel after the
reading can cause you to misinterpret the work you've
done. Analyzing is intellectual, and we want to avoid

that at all costs, especially in the time immediately after you read your letter. That time is liable to be filled with emotion, even if you're not consciously aware of it. As with anything new that you do, it will take a while for the full impact to sink in. Be careful not to presume that what you feel right after the reading represents anything other than your feelings at that moment.

Starting very shortly after reading your letter, you may begin to remember other things, both positive and negative, from the relationship. In the next chapter we'll tell you how to deal with those new discoveries.

Now go find a listener and read your letter.

CHAPTER THIRTEEN

WHAT ABOUT NEW DISCOVERIES?

As the result of doing your review and letter, you've cleaned a great deal of the baggage out of your emotional attic. You will probably recall other events, both positive and negative, that you'll want to complete as soon as you become aware of them. It's really very simple, all you have to do is write a short PS letter.

Dear Fred,
    PS: I just remembered something else that I want to say to you. I remember the time that you told some of your friends that I wasn't a good cook, while I was sitting right there. I was

so embarrassed, I wanted to die. I forgive you
for that insensitive and unnecessary comment.
I forgive you so I can be free.

    I have to go now and let go of the pain.

    Good-bye, Fred.

The PS letter could contain a forgiveness for a
painful thing like the one we just showed. Or it could
be an apology for something positive you never told
your partner. "I'm sorry I never told you how much I
appreciated how sweet you were with my grandparents." Again, always close and complete the letter with
"good-bye." You can do little PS letters as often as you
think of things that need to be completed. As soon as
possible after you've written them, make sure you read
them aloud to a safe person. Don't miss that last step;
it's really important.

    Important note: Communication of a completion
letter is a private and confidential matter. As we've
stated, forgiveness and negative emotional statements
must never be made directly to living people. The shortened version of Russell's letter was presented only to
illustrate what you must do. A completion letter should
never be sent or read to the person it's addressed to.

Completion Doesn't Mean You'll Never Be Sad Again

Completion means that you have effectively communicated everything you have identified that was unfinished

for you up until this moment, in all aspects of the relationship that you just worked on. It doesn't mean that you will never be sad again, any more than you would never be happy again. Nor does it mean that you will never miss your former partner. In fact, you may experience a great deal of emotion. It's very likely that you had been pushing your feelings down for a long time.

Completion allows you a full range of human emotions that attach to your memory of someone. **Completion also means that you don't have to sabotage your new relationship by holding back your trust out of fear of getting hurt again**.

Is One Review and Letter Enough?

There's a strong possibility that you will feel a sense of relief as the result of the work you've done so far. That's a mixed blessing. While you may feel good right now, it can give you the false idea that you're totally done. Of course, if you've only been in one romantic relationship that ended, then you only have to make one review and write and read one completion letter. But if you've been in more than one, you need to do a separate review and completion letter for each one. We encourage you to go back and complete all of them. Let us rephrase that and be more commanding. **Go back and complete all of your other incomplete romantic relationships. Do it very soon**.

Since you are the common denominator in each relationship, reviewing them the way we showed you gives you a more honest picture of yourself. You'll get to see your habits and patterns more clearly than if you just talk about and analyze yourself. This new vision, coupled with your new emotional completeness, is what allows you to change. In fact, it will probably compel you to change. It will no longer be comfortable for you to stay the way you were as it relates to making the same errors over and over. That includes the major error of overriding your intuition.

Make sure you save your romantic relationship history to remind you of the relationships you still need to review. Write a relationship review and a completion letter for each person on the list. It's a good idea to separate the writing of each review and letter by a couple of days, so the relationships don't get jumbled in your head and heart. If circumstances allow, get together with your listener each time you've finished a letter and read it.

Your New Emotional Survival Kit

Is it possible that you will get hurt emotionally again? Yes. We all know that our partners could be struck down by an accident or die from an illness. If something tragic like that were to happen, any of us would be devastated. But we cannot allow those possibilities to make us withhold our affection and commitment.

We also have no guarantee that when we get home at the end of the day our partner will still love us and want to be with us. We can't even be sure that we will still love our partner. The divorce rate hovering at or near 50 percent stands in stark testimony to that sad reality. Again, even though people and relationships can change, we must not allow that possibility to make us withhold our affection and commitment. If we do that, we run the risk of creating the very ending we fear most.

There is good news. Having taken the actions in this book, and being willing to finish the job by completing your other incomplete relationships, actually gives you a guarantee. You now know that if the worst possible thing should happen and circumstances ended your new relationship, you would have the actions of this book to help you complete the pain. There is no guarantee that when you begin dating someone new the relationship will be successful. But this time you can be sure that you will not sabotage potential happiness by your fear of getting hurt again. Having this emotional tool kit will give you the freedom to love openly and fully. It will allow you to trust yourself and your intuition.

Your Past Is Complete but Not Forgotten

Becoming emotionally complete does not mean that your memory has been terminated. In your day-to-day life, there may be reminders of your relationships with former partners. Some of the reminders will be conscious and obvious, others not. Your memories of those relationships will come with emotions attached. Some of your feelings will be happy, fond, and joyful. Some will be negative, sad, and uncomfortable. This is normal. Don't fight it, just allow it. If you try to hide or bury those feelings, they will continue to harm you. **If you allow negative feelings to occur without resistance, they will go away**.

As you begin a new relationship, there will be inevitable comparisons to other relationships. Your mind will generate thoughts and feelings as it looks back at your former relationships and holds them up to the new one. It's impossible not to do that. You just need to recognize that those thoughts and feelings are also normal. However, feelings are not a call to action or an indication that you shouldn't be in the new relationship. Our minds are tricky. They often want us to go back to someone or something familiar. Our minds don't like newness or change.

Carry-on Luggage Only

We started this book with the silly but accurate metaphor about emotional baggage. We'll end this section with another bit of silliness. As a result of the actions you've taken, you can now travel with carry-on luggage only. You will not have to check mountains of trunks, suitcases, and valises filled with your past when you board your next relationship flight. Perhaps you can now find that nonstop ticket to happiness.

PART III

A New Beginning

We'd like to acknowledge the courage and effort you've put forth up to this point. We know that the things we asked you to do aren't easy. But easy almost never leads to better. Before you jump back into the relationship jungle there are some things you need to learn so you can be successful. Please give this section of the book the same attention you gave the preceding sections.

It's one thing to take the actions in this book and become emotionally complete in your prior relationships. It's another for you to start doing things differently. The fact that you have done what we've asked doesn't mean that you have changed what you do and how you will react in new situations. This part of the book is dedicated to teaching you practical tools. They will help you make real changes and sustain them in your relationships. To complete your past you had to take the specific actions we laid out. We're now going to show you how to do the same with some of the habits that have limited you. We will also teach you how to rebuild trust in your intuition. And we'll show you how to establish the criteria that are most important for you in choosing your mate.

CHAPTER FOURTEEN

HABITS:
OFF WITH THE OLD,
ON WITH THE NEW

e are all creatures of habit. From early childhood we begin developing habits in response to what we're taught. One of the earliest habits we're taught is how to brush our teeth. Our parents teach us this important habit so we'll be able to maintain good dental health. You probably don't remember your early training in toothbrushing, but chances are you do it today the way it was taught to you many years ago. You practiced what you learned until it became a habit.

When we take piano lessons, we practice playing the scales until our fingers develop habits. We are eventually able to do it without looking at the keys. The same thing happens in sports. When we practice throwing a baseball, we learn to make that action automatically without having to think about each of the individual movements. What develops is called "muscle memory."

Emotional Muscle Memory

We also develop habits in reaction to what happens with the people in our lives. As we repeat those habits, we develop an *emotional muscle memory* that becomes automatic. Many of those habits are good and are worth keeping. But some aren't. We're going to focus on the bad habits so we can replace them with good ones. Bad habits don't go away by themselves. You can't just think a habit away or wish it away. Nor can you superimpose a new affirmative idea on top of an old one and think the earlier one will disappear. So many self-help books fall short because they lead you to believe that merely identifying a problem is all you have to do and the solution is automatic. But it's not. That half measure leaves people unchanged and more and more frustrated.

Building new habits on top of old ones is a setup for failure. The best way to look at it is to think about a room that needs painting. The paint is cracked and peeling and there are holes in the plaster. You wouldn't try to apply new paint over a surface like that. It wouldn't hold. What you would do first is strip away the old paint. Then you'd fill the cracks with fresh plaster. Next you'd sand it until it was smooth, and then you would apply the new paint.

That's exactly what we've asked you to do as it relates to prior relationships. We asked you to strip the flaking, discolored paint off old memories so you could identify and complete unfinished emotional business. Having done that, you're now ready for a new coat of paint that will consist of some new habits. As you set about building these new habits, keep in mind that your brain will still want to be "right" about all of its old habits. Those habits are tied to your prior relationships. Completing old relationships and building new habits are interconnected. The application of both is what allows you to overcome the default setting of "rightness" that leads you back to old habits.

Developing a new habit to replace an old one requires three things:

1. You must first become aware of the need to acquire a new habit.

2. You must then discover or be taught the components of the new habit in their proper order.

3. And finally, you must then practice the new components in their proper order approximately thirty-five to forty times. Then you will be the proud possessor of a new habit.

Here's that three-part idea with a positive result:

1. Russell had become aware that he had a habit of reacting defensively when Alice suggested that his shirt and pants didn't match. Alice told him that he reacted like a schoolboy who was being punished. Russell always argued with Alice about that. One day it dawned on him that the habit of reacting that way had nothing to do with Alice. It had to do with the way his dad had sometimes talked to him when he was a child.

2. With his new awareness, Russell had to learn to stop whenever Alice made a suggestion about his clothing and ask himself a few questions. "Does she look like my father? Am I five years old, and is it 1948? And most of all, is she right?" The answers were no, no, no, and yes.

2. He practiced and practiced. Each time Alice commented on his outfit, he'd ask himself those questions. As a result, he now has a wonderful new habit. Sometimes he looks at Alice and says, "It's not 1948 and you're not my dad." Alice laughs every time. Then he does as she has suggested.

As Russell developed that new habit, he was able to apply it in other areas. As a result, Alice found it easier to talk to him about things that used to be difficult. It has expanded their relationship. You may not believe this, but Russell will now ask Alice for guidance when he has to dress in anything other than blue jeans and golf shirts.

Rebuilding Your Intuition

In addition to establishing new habits, you must rebuild your intuition so that it will again be a valuable asset in your life. Most of us have learned to distrust our intuition. We have practiced distrusting our intuition until it has become a habit. Sadly, that distrust contributes to the formalizing of many relationships that were never meant to be. When we play a game like *Trivial Pursuit* or play along with the contestants on *Jeopardy*, we see the value of intuition in answering the questions. How often have you not gone with your first answer and later discovered that it was right? That's when you ask, "Why didn't I trust my gut?"

Very early in the book, we mentioned that a large percentage of the people we've helped over the years had told us that they'd overridden their intuition when deciding whether to begin or stay in a relationship. The most common complaint they made to us was, "Why didn't I trust my gut?" If you want to reconnect to your ability to trust your gut, here's a three-part example for learning to trust your intuition:

1. Once in a while you might remember a friend of yours from high school. An image of that person just pops into your mind. You may not have any idea of what caused you to think of that person, and it's not necessary to know. You might have an impulse to call or e-mail that person. But like most people, you may just let it slide by without taking any action on it. We want you to develop a new habit in response to those kinds of memories and the impulses that often accompany them.

2. What are the components of this new adventure? This one's really simple. Pick up the phone or go to your computer. Take the action that follows the memory and the impulse, and contact the person you thought of. If you use the phone, when they answer or when their machine answers say, "You popped into my mind this morning and I just wanted to say hi." And then follow whatever thread the conversation takes. If you use e-mail, say the same thing, and then see if any response comes back to you. If and when it does, follow that thread wherever it goes.

3. You are on the way to developing a new habit. Instead of pushing the memory and impulse aside, follow them. Doing it the first time may be a little scary, but don't let that stop you. It will be the beginning of developing a new habit that will expand your ability to respond to your intuitive voice. If you persevere, astonishing things will begin to happen. You will be amazed.

The day will come when you are totally reconnected to your most wonderful gift—your intuition. The key is allowing yourself to listen to and trust the *little voice*. Used properly, it is your greatest ally in making important decisions. This is especially true as it relates to choosing the person you will spend the rest of your life with.

John has practiced trusting his intuition for many years. Here's a story of his that illustrates the benefit of learning to follow your intuitive instincts:

I almost always follow the little voice now. Sometimes I find out later what it was about and sometimes I don't, but I don't question it.

Some years ago the image of an old friend from college popped into my mind. I picked up the phone and called him. After a brief conversation getting caught up with our lives, **something prompted me to ask him if anything was troubling him.** *There definitely was. So much so, that he was contemplating taking his own life. He told me he was trapped in a job he hated and deeply in debt. He thought that if he told his wife, she would leave him. He felt as if there was no way out.*

As we talked he told me that much of his early life had been spent making decisions to please his parents. With that, he had developed a major habit of seeking approval. He'd always wanted to be a veterinarian, but his parents suggested a different career path. Instead of following his own instincts, he did what they wanted. The end result was the state of despair he was in when I called him.

I was able to guide him to complete his relationships with each of his parents so that he could make some new choices. After doing that, and with the agreement and support of his wife, he decided to go back to school and follow the dream he'd had since he was seven years old. He now has a thriving veterinary practice. He is very happy and so are his wife and children.

NEW COMMUNICATION HABITS

C ountless books, articles, and research papers indicate that many romantic relationships fail because of poor communication. To say that effective communication is the key to all successful human relationships would be an understatement. The number one factor cited by most people after a relationship fails is that they didn't believe their partner had actually heard them. Therefore, they felt misunderstood. This is true of men and women of all ages. With this as a backdrop, it's a good idea to learn better habits for hearing and understanding the partner you will share your life with.

Inbound Communication—
The Most Important Part

The primary reason that most people don't feel heard is the lack of awareness about the directions in which communications flow. Effective communication involves two directions, outbound and inbound. Unfortunately, we are trained in only one of them—outbound. We learn to project our voices to be heard and to moderate our tone so as not to be monotonous. We learn to enunciate clearly and to make eye contact and to be aware of using the right amount of hand gestures. These are all very valuable skills for the outbound aspect of communication.

But how many classes have you ever had in Inbound Communication? What were you taught about listening effectively to what others are saying? Most people draw a blank when asked those questions. Yet the key to communication is hearing and understanding what the other person means. It is much more important than most outbound skills in helping couples communicate with each other.

One of the unique things about verbal interactions is that meaningful communications are often delivered in two parts. The first part is usually the lead-in, and the second part contains the important material. An example might be when a couple has planned to go to the movies. But when that day arrives, one of the couple has had a particularly difficult time at work. When the other partner gets home, he or she says, "What time are we going to the movie?" So far so good. But the reply has the possibility of starting a misunderstanding or an argument.

Here's the reply: "Let's go tomorrow; I've had a really tough day."

In a perfect world, the speaker delivers his or her information while the listener pays full attention. After hearing what was said, the listener then responds. This makes sense and works well if both parties listen effectively. But therein lies the rub. Most people stop listening as soon as they hear the first part of the communication. Imagine if the listener stops listening and starts preparing a reply before the speaker has even finished. Nothing good can happen. Not only does the speaker not feel heard but the listener's response will always be to the wrong part of the communication.

In our example, the mate hears only the "let's go tomorrow" part. He or she doesn't actually hear the "I've had a really tough day" part. And to make matters worse, responds with, "But we had a plan." Or "I've been looking forward to that movie for a week." The battle starts here. Our first person doesn't feel heard. He or she senses that the partner hadn't been listening. It also might remind the first person of parallel events with prior partners. He or she also goes "out of the moment" in fear of the repeat of something that never felt good. The individuals within couples develop hair-trigger responses in these kinds of interactions. An argument can erupt in a heartbeat.

We doubt that anyone reading this hasn't been on both sides of this battle. Rarely can either half of a couple tell exactly what started an argument. Their stories are always wildly different. An independent observer would go crazy trying to figure out who did what to whom without a videotape of the fight. Even the video would be of limited value if the referee didn't spot the premature answer from the listener. When relationship battles are engaged, both participants usually wind up "out of the moment," and both use past relationship problems to guide them. Ultimately, there can be only one conclusion to this constant bickering: the relationship will end. With that potential, we cannot overemphasize the importance of improving your listening ability. Effective listening is the most crucial new habit you must develop.

Here's a Better Way

Let's replay the situation about the movie and show you a better way:

First partner: "What time are we going to the movie?"

Second partner: "Let's go tomorrow; **I've had a really tough day.**"

First partner: "Yeah, you sound exhausted. I'm a little disappointed, but let's try again for tomorrow."

Second partner: "Thanks, honey; I really need to chill tonight."

Sometimes, as in that scenario, it will make sense to modify plans. Although the second partner was disappointed, it was not a big deal. More often than not, all that is required from the listening partner is an acknowledgment of the statement. For example, if your partner has just told you some good news from work, your response would be, "How exciting." If it was bad news, you might say, "How frustrating."

Collision Courses

Effective communication is complicated by the belief system we discussed earlier. The human mind believes that what it believes is always right. In conversations with your mate, when you stop listening and begin preparing your response, it will be based on your rightness. You are not the only one who does that. When the tables are turned, your partner usually does the same thing.

One of the maddening elements of the inbound communication problem is that both partners do it to each other. Neither partner realizes that they are doing the very thing they hate when it is done to them. The killer factor is that this demolition derby becomes a habit of the relationship. And like all habits, it keeps wanting to repeat itself even though the consequences are terrible, each and every time.

When one partner realizes that the other isn't really listening, he or she will go "out of the moment," in fear of a repeat of something that has happened before. At that point both partners are not present in real time. Most arguments start from that position. When the argument starts it will be based on each partner thinking they are "right" and the other is "wrong." It is the ultimate no-win situation. As individuals have habits, so do couples, and this one is a relationship killer.

You Might Listen, but You Don't Hear Me!

We've rarely met anyone who hasn't said or felt that their partner didn't hear them. When they say that to their partner, the response is almost always, "I heard every word." He or she then repeats what you said, verbatim. But even when they can do that, you still don't believe they heard you. It was because you'd noticed that they were no longer listening after the first part. They were preparing a response. The real complaint is that although they may be listening, they are not **hearing and understanding** what you are trying to say.

We've talked to thousands of couples in which both partners report not having felt understood. To correct this problem, you must use your new habit-building tools in a specific area—**listening**—with the goal of really hearing and understanding your partner. Here's one way to begin developing that new habit:

Follow their words in your head as they speak them.

When your mate is talking, follow the words just as you would follow a bouncing ball or as you would concentrate as a news crawler goes across the bottom of a TV screen. Concentrate! **Give no thought to what your reply will be**. Just practice following their words in your head as they speak them. Practice, practice, practice, and then practice some more. You can practice this everywhere. It's not limited to your mate. Practice at work and in social situations. All you have to remember is the image of the bouncing ball. When you listen this way, you actually have a chance of understanding what your partner is trying to say. By listening effectively, you will also realize that until a question has been asked, there is no need for you to go off and find an answer. Yes, the subject the other person is talking about will stimulate your brain to look for what it knows on that topic. Don't formulate a reply until the other person is finished.

Finally, as hard as it is to believe, you will have your chance to speak! Let us repeat that. You will have your chance to speak. You will also have an opportunity to answer a question if one has been asked. As you listen and really hear your partner, you will build more and more trust and safety within the relationship.

Seeing Is Believing

Most experts indicate that nonverbal communication is the largest aspect of the exchange of thoughts and feelings. Because this is true, we place higher value on that element of communication. Some of the nonverbal communication is in the form of facial gestures and body language, and some is in tone of voice. It's important to have a conscious awareness of your nonverbal listening habits. Making faces, especially disapproving ones, while your partner is talking will set a tone and attitude that can cause big problems. Since a huge percentage of your ability to communicate is nonverbal, you may need to develop and practice some new habits in that part of your listening.

Again, we cannot overemphasize the importance of improving all of your listening skills. Once you are in a new relationship, your ability to listen and hear will help you establish your love for your new partner. Every chance you get to listen to someone speaking, we want you to practice these new skills. You may be surprised at how quickly the new habit develops, and you'll be thrilled at the enhancement it will bring to all your relationships. **Start practicing these new listening skills today.**

Right or Happy—Pick One

Let's move away from the mechanical issues of communication and go to content. Another problem that relationships face is each partner's need to be right. It all goes back to the belief system we mentioned in chapter 1. The human mind believes that what it knows is "always right." If I'm right and you don't agree with me, then you must be wrong. Out in the real world, this is the stuff wars are made of. If you think that's an exaggeration, pick up a newspaper or watch the news and see how many hot spots there are on this globe. People are fighting and dying over ideological belief systems. **I'm right; you're wrong; we fight to the death**. We don't mean to make light of this phenomenon. But we must use it to make the obvious connection to romantic relationships. That means that each person in a couple believes he or she is right. In the end, it looks like this: **I'm right; you're wrong; we fight until we break up**.

Luckily, it's not too late to teach old dogs new tricks. Anytime you sense yourself feeling "right" in an argument with your mate, you would be well advised to stop and ask yourself a question: "Do I want to be right, or do I want to be happy?" If you're like we used to be, you probably thought that being right was being happy. By now you've probably learned that being right is liable to make you alone, not happy.

Before we go on, let us clarify something. We're not suggesting that you compromise anything you hold to be important. We're not suggesting that you become a doormat or that you need to be a dummy. In fact, it's not really about right or wrong or smart or stupid. It's only about recognizing your brain's overdeveloped need to be right, no matter the cost.

The other powerful lesson in this section is to realize that you and your mates—past, present, or future—all share the same condition of "terminal rightness."

Every argument you've ever had, without exception, is based on opposing rightness. Your partner always feels as right as you do. Can you both be right? *Yes!* Otherwise there would never be any arguments. Think about that for a minute.

In a Crisis We Go Back to Old Beliefs

When relationship battles are engaged, both participants usually wind up "out of the moment." They each use past relationship problems to guide them. Unfortunately, most of the memories of past problems don't contain solutions. Ultimately, there can be only one conclusion to this constant bickering: the relationship must end.

When a crisis occurs, our mind looks for the information it has stored about dealing with the current problem. More often than not, it finds obsolete and unhelpful ideas. This is the danger zone in which we make our memorized rightness the answer to the situation. In the meantime, our partner is doing the equal and opposite, from his or her past.

Mom or Dad or Just Familiar?

Although it does not fall directly under the heading of new communication habits, there's something we'd like to point out that you may find helpful. There is a common misconception that suggests that people marry their mother or father. It's one of those clichés that seems to have a ring of truth but isn't really accurate. As we have all adopted more and more of the psychological language that is part of our times, we are tempted to fit everything in a convenient slot like that. But it's much more realistic to suggest that we are attracted to what is familiar to us. So it's not necessarily Mom or Dad but aspects of either or both that are familiar to us that we unconsciously seek in our mates. The danger in that attraction is that familiar isn't always good, it's just familiar. As a result of doing all the work we've suggested, you may become aware of some of those areas where you've let familiar guide you even when it has caused you to repeat bad choices.

One of the benefits of the work you've done in this book is that you will be able to develop new beliefs to replace the obsolete ones that have limited you. The old beliefs are habits just like everything else you do. Keep in mind that just having a new idea does not make it a new habit. You must practice and practice. The same is true for new beliefs.

CHAPTER SIXTEEN

WATERING PLASTIC FLOWERS

After relationships end, there often comes a point when we get slapped in the face with a hard dose of reality. We become painfully aware that we've been doing the same things over and over and then acting disappointed when we get the same results. There are many clichés that express this common occurrence. Most people have heard the one about "throwing a bucket into an empty well and being surprised when there's no water." Our personal favorite is "watering plastic flowers." In fact, we even considered it as the title for this book. The wit and sarcasm of it are so clear, yet so many people keep doing what they do and getting what they get and then acting surprised.

Uncharted Waters

From here on you'll be in uncharted waters. One of the crucial areas where we tend to repeat bad habits is the criteria we use to choose our mates. In the previous chapter we talked about how to develop new, life-affirming habits. Some of the old criteria you have used to choose your mates have become habits that must be changed. When you do new and unfamiliar things, your mind will try to resist and drag you back to the familiar old ideas. This part of your journey will require a great deal of self-discipline as well as absolute honesty.

The mind defends against new ideas by sending messages that the new thing is uncomfortable. It's common to interpret *uncomfortable* to mean *bad* or even to take it to mean that it's intuitively incorrect. But neither of those is necessarily so. You must work your way through both the discomfort and the unfamiliarity that are caused by the new action. As an example: Most people in today's world have a computer and use a mouse to navigate. Can you remember when you first tried to use a mouse? Do you remember how awkward it was at first to manipulate the device and get the arrow where you wanted it? Now you are so proficient with the mouse that you never even think about it; you just do it.

As you understand the idea of moving from unfamiliar to familiar, it will be easier for you to overcome the trap of staying stuck in the old ideas you've been using. With that in mind, we're going to show you how to formulate a new plan of action. You're going to have to practice it rigorously until the new actions don't feel quite so unfamiliar.

Dating and courtship are complex. The mixture of physiological, emotional, and intuitive matters can be confusing even to the most orderly person. We also cannot overlook the social pressures applied by peers, family, and others. At the time we most need our wits about us, it can often seem that logic and reason are in short supply. That's okay. Love is not logical or reasonable. Love is love. Even though love is not logical, we still need to be able to make choices that are based on what is true for ourselves. We need to have some basic criteria that will guide us in choosing a life mate.

Plan—What Plan?

Twenty-seven years ago John found himself facing a familiar dilemma. He had just experienced yet another relationship breakup and was determined *not* to make the same mistake one more time. His story makes it clear that it is possible to do something new and get a better result.

I had just experienced yet another breakup of a relationship. The woman and I had worked diligently to try and make this one succeed. But it didn't make it. One more time

I found myself confused and alone. And again, the thing I truly wanted had eluded me.

I am a great believer in putting pencil to paper. I've discovered that writing things down helps me achieve clarity. And so there I was at the kitchen table, pencil in hand, preparing to examine what had happened. As I began to reflect, I realized that I was simply writing down many of the same things I had written down after my last breakup. The more I thought, the more it became obvious that the issues that had caused this breakup were the same as in most of the previous breakups. Undoubtedly there was a pattern. But what exactly was it?

Try as I might, I couldn't figure out the pattern. I kept thinking and rethinking the same things over and over. I was stumped. So I invoked another skill that has helped me throughout my life. I decided to shelve the search for a while. I was in the middle of the forest and couldn't see for all the trees. I gave the writing a rest for a couple of days. During that time I would occasionally become aware that I was looking for clues to the puzzle. I also suspect that my subconscious was on the job too, searching through my past for the answers.

*Awareness comes from different places and in many forms. Sometimes it comes as a flash thought. Other times it comes from a friend or stranger whose words are overheard. I can't really say where my new awareness came from; I don't remember. But the idea was very clear. **The idea was to back up a step in the process**. So I decided that rather than just looking at past relationships that had failed I'd now look at how I was picking the people I'd been in relationships* with. My new idea was to try and pinpoint what criteria I was using to select the people I dated. So I grabbed my trusty pen and pad and started over again.

Across the top of the page I wrote, "Dating Criteria."

Next I wrote the number 1 near the left-hand margin. Then I started to ask myself what was it about the last few women I had been involved with that attracted me to them. The first entry was easy:

1. Good looking

Then I wrote down the number 2. So far I had the following:

1. Good looking
2. *(And this is where I hit a snag.)*

I thought and thought. I racked my brain. I got up and walked around my apartment. Soon I was dumbfounded. I remember thinking, "This can't be true." But the fact remained, **there was no number 2.**

It was a "big-time revelation" moment. Many questions were answered by the fact that there was no number 2. "How could this be?" Where had I ever gotten the idea that good looks were enough to build a relationship around? Again I decided to put the pad and pencil down for a while. For the next several days I looked around me. I watched television. I went to some social events. In the end I realized something very simple. There's nothing wrong with good looks, but good looks alone is certainly not enough. I remember laughing at myself, thinking how utterly stupid I had been for most of my life.

I took a chance and began to talk with some women friends. I asked them what were the exact criteria they were using to pick the people they went out with. Surprise, surprise. They had never thought about the question either. When I asked them to think about their last two or three relationships, they too discovered that whatever their criteria had been they were neither accurate nor helpful for them.

A dear woman friend of mine tells a story on herself. "I was between relationships when I walked into a convenience store one night. As I was looking for the things I needed, I spied what I thought was a man at the end of the aisle. I saw cowboy boots, very tight jeans, a worn leather jacket, and long flowing hair halfway down the back of the jacket. I remember thinking, 'I gotta have that.' But then I remembered that I was in the process of working on new dating criteria. I stopped. I actually laughed out loud at myself. Here I was about to try and bump into this person to strike up a conversation and I hadn't even seen his face. In truth I didn't even know for sure if it was a man or a woman. I turned and left the store vowing that I would keep working on this stuff no matter how long it took."

I could fully identify with my friend's story. By this point I too was becoming very clear that the singular "looks good" criterion was at the root of the problem. But discovering the problem did not create the solution. The unanswered question was, "What criteria should I be using?"

First Try—Wrong Turn—Dead End

Next I made a wrong turn. I went down a road that was a dead end. Thank goodness I saw the error before I took action. My first attempt at coming up with a solution to improve the criteria I would use for future dating was about as off the mark as it could have been. I made a list of what I wanted in the *other person. It was a very detailed list.*

She had to be the following:

> *good looking*
> *well-read*
> *sexually compatible*
> *interested in current events*
> *funny*
> *able to make me laugh*
> *supportive*

The list went on and on, kind of like a child's wish list. As I looked at the list, I sensed that something was wrong and it wouldn't work. I stared at the list until it hit me. This time I had one of those lightning-bolt flashes. I realized that my list **was based entirely on the concept that someone else's attributes were 100 percent responsible for me finding the right person and making me happy.** *It was a set of criteria that was completely outside my control. It was at best like shooting craps in Vegas.*

It was also enormously arrogant of me. The idea that I could set up such a gauntlet for someone else to run was preposterous. And in the final analysis, that criteria list was completely intellectual.

Back to the Drawing Board

After careful consideration, it became clear to me that a better approach would be to start with me. What was important to me, about me? What were the things about me that I would not compromise? What were the things that were important enough to me that I should at least be aware of them in advance, so they wouldn't surprise me later?

I also knew that if this new plan were to work, it would have to be based on the truth. The truth about me. So, what was my truth? I had to start all over.

The "New" New Criteria

1. *Physically attractive (to me).*

What constitutes good looks? There's no single answer. There's not even a single answer for any one person. Nevertheless there's always something that attracts our first glance or look. There's always something about a person, usually visual or verbal, that causes us to want to meet them. My best friend may not think the person I'm attracted to is good looking. So this is a personal issue for each of us.

After writing that down I found the first new piece to my personal puzzle.

In 1975, my daughter was born. Several years later my wife and I lost a son shortly after his birth. A huge percentage of marriages that experience child loss end in divorce. That is what happened to ours. After the dust of the separation and divorce settled, I made a solemn vow that my daughter would always be a part of my life.

Now my new plan had two items:

1 *Physically attractive (to me).*
2. *My daughter must be part of my life.*

Another piece of truth about me is that I am an old jock. I like to watch sports. I like to attend games. I like to coach kids. I could honestly say that I did not see myself ever changing that. So it went on the list:

1. *Physically attractive (to me).*
2. *My daughter must be part of my life.*
3. *Sports are important to me.*

By now I realized that I was on a very important search. It was getting easier. The search was about me and who I was. Truth is very important to me. So I added it to the new list:

1. *Physically attractive (to me).*
2. *My daughter must be part of my life.*
3. *Sports are important to me.*
4. *Truth is essential to me.*

When I go to a party, I like the freedom to roam around and talk to a lot of people. I've been uncomfortable with women who would attach themselves to me the whole evening, making me responsible for them, kind of like a babysitter. I realized that any woman I might share my life with would have to be able to make conversation with others:

1. *Physically attractive (to me).*
2. *My daughter must be part of my life.*
3. *Sports are important to me.*
4. *Truth is essential to me.*
5. *No babysitting.*

I was on a roll. Then I stopped and thought that I'd better road test my new plan to make sure I was on the right track. The new plan was very simple. I decided that when I saw someone that I was attracted to, I would ask her out to coffee. No date, just coffee. Obviously, before asking for the coffee date, I had already made my personal decision that she was good looking—to me. During that first meeting we would simply talk and see if we had anything in common. Then I would listen for my intuitive voice. I would also try to be very honest with myself.

One example was a model that I met and went to coffee with. After an hour and a half it was clear to me that the only topic she could talk about was fashion. Please hear me when I say there is nothing wrong with fashion. But it wasn't right for me. So in this case, even though I found her very attractive, there was no second coffee.

Before I had this new set of criteria, I had tried the approach that relied on looks only many times and it had always failed. At the very least I was getting a little smarter at not going past early interactions that were clearly not destined to have a future.

Although this new plan might sound simple and easy, it was not without its frustrations. After about five first-coffee dates that didn't lead to a second one, I began to think my plan would not work. But fortunately, I also thought that five examples might not be enough. So I carried on.

As time went on, there were quite a few second coffees. The conversations that led to coffee number two were great. In fact, several of the women were interested in things that I also found interesting yet were new to me. This led to me visiting book stores and learning about topics with which I had no previous experience. It might seem like I was drinking an awful lot of coffee, and you might have begun to wonder if there were ever any first dates. Yes, there were quite a few. And every first date involved my daughter. If indeed she were number two on my list of truths about me, then there was no reason for my beautiful daughter to come as a later surprise to anyone.

How did these first dates work out? I was amazed. Amazed by the number of women who put themselves in competition with a four-year-old. In those cases there was no second date. I also need to say that I called each of these women and told them that I thought they were truly nice people but that I didn't feel as if we were right for each other in a long-term relationship. I was amazed at how many of those women thanked me for that simple courtesy. I also made some new and very dear friends.

There were several second dates. These always involved a sports event of some kind. A baseball game, a hockey game, or some other large spectator event. It's enough to say that some people like sports events and some don't. There were even some third dates that involved parties. I would always take my date around and introduce her to many people and then excuse myself to go and have a conversation with someone else. Some of these women would fall right into the theme of the evening's party and make new friends and carry on conversations throughout the night.

(Before I go on, I want to make a comment. It could seem as if everything that was happening was entirely based on me and what I wanted and needed. That's not true. Many of the women I met were also trying to find out what was true for them and which of their own criteria were most important. It was not a one-way street. As I mentioned, I learned about many new things as this process unfolded.)

Were there any who were right? In fact, there were two. In both cases I thought long and hard about formalizing a relationship. During this whole period of about two years I was also working hard on one of the other things mentioned in this book—intuition. I tried to listen to it and not disregard the small messages that came to me. Several dramatic examples of following these intuitive pieces of information helped me begin to learn to trust my intuition again. As sad as it was each time, I realized that both of the women who seemed to be a match for me were not. Intuitively I knew the relationships were wrong for me. I had long and sad conver-

sations with each of them as I did not want to lead them on. We're still friends to this day.

I Took Completion Actions before Starting Over

There was heartache in each of those two breakups. But because I help others deal with the pain caused by endings, I know to take the actions I teach, which are the ones outlined in the beginning of this book. It was essential that I complete my relationship with each woman before dating again. So I did.

In spite of those near misses, I had a sense that something important was going to happen. I was changing in a very positive way. My dual quest for the discovery of my truth and someone to share my life with was actually working, although the latter had not yet been achieved. I was feeling hopeful.

I Thought You'd Never Ask

Occasionally someone asks me how my wife and I got together. I thought you'd never ask. Here's the rest of my story:

*One night I was standing in a parking lot talking with an old, dear friend. We were just catching up on life as we hadn't seen each other for some time. About ten minutes into the conversation a woman friend of hers came walking up. We were introduced, and the three of us chatted for a while. **And I knew!** Knew? Yes, I heard an intuitive voice in my head saying, "**This is the person who is right for you.**" That little*

*meeting and conversation ended and we all went our separate
ways. But I couldn't get her out of my mind.*

*While I had been working hard at reestablishing trust in
my intuition, I also felt that I should keep going with my new
plan of action. I needed to make sure that my intuition and
feelings were correct. So I called up this beautiful woman
(remember the "attractive to me" criterion) and invited her to
coffee. The conversation went really well. A couple of days
later we had another coffee date. Again, I found that we had
many things in common and at the same time we were
delightfully different.*

Send in the Clowns

*Several days later I called and asked her if she would like to go
on a triple date. I told her we would be going to a wildly exciting event with my daughter. I'm sure I oversold the evening, but
I wanted her to say yes. I finally told her we were going to the
circus. We met for dinner and an amazing thing happened.*
**After about five minutes she and my daughter could not
have cared less whether I was with them.** *After dinner, we
went to the circus. Throughout the evening, they were
enthralled with each other and having the times of their lives.*

*Our next date was to a Dodger game. This woman, while
born in the United States, had been raised in Canada and
had never been to a baseball game.* We talked and laughed,*

---

*You Can Take the Girl out of the Theater
My wife is an Emmy Award–winning actress. Theater is her life
and has been since she was a little girl. When our son, Cole,

and I was busy praying that the game would go into extra innings. I was in heaven. And even though I was 100 percent certain that she was a person who was right for me, I still continued with my plan. On our next date, we went to a party in Westwood. Shortly after we got there, just as I was about to give her my little talk about introducing her to some people and then going our separate ways for a while, she turned to me and said, "I'm going to visit with some of my friends. Let's meet back here in an hour." I could have kissed her; I think I did.

We continued to date for several months. My intuitive voice kept saying everything was okay. Everything felt right. Eight months later we were married.

So what happened? It's now twenty-seven years later and we are closer and more considerate and in love than ever before. Looks like the new plan worked very well.

---

was playing baseball, I was one of the volunteer coaches for the team. If you recall, the third entry on my personal truth list was my involvement in sports. But my wife, who is of the theater and unfamiliar with baseball, has applied her own unique blend to the two activities. When Cole was going off to baseball practice she would say, "Have a nice rehearsal, honey." And when he'd get home in his dirty uniform, she'd say, "Please put your dirty costume in the hamper." As they might say, "You can take the girl out of the theater, but you can't take the theater out of the girl."

CHAPTER SEVENTEEN

YOU NEED A PLAN— START NOW

J ohn's plan worked because it was based on what was true for him. It worked because he had taken the actions to complete what was unfinished for him in prior relationships, which helped him see what his truths were. And it worked because John had learned to trust his intuition.

Now would be the perfect time for you to write down your criteria and make a new plan based on what is true for you. As you begin, you too will have to start trusting your intuitive sense of what is important for you.

Remember, just reading this book is not enough. Make sure you take the actions. They are the key that will open your heart and let you love, and be loved, again. John's and Russell's success stories didn't happen overnight. You too will have to be courageous, diligent, and patient. The actions in this book have worked for thousands of people. Of course we cannot guarantee that you'll find the person of your dreams. We can only guarantee that if you take the actions we've outlined, you can become the person you really are and therefore be available to be in a loving, trusting relationship.

Don't wait, do it now.

Postscript

What about Other Kinds of Relationships?

It may be obvious to you at this point that your romantic relationships are *not* the entire cause of the habits and behaviors you brought with you into those relationships. You may now have a clear sense that you have some cumulative incompleteness with either or both of your parents or siblings or other important people in your life. This would be an ideal time to go back and complete what is emotionally unfinished for you in those relationships. Some of the people who affected you may still be living, others not. Either way, it's important that you become complete with them so you don't drag the baggage from that section of your little red wagon into your current or next romantic relationship.

The actions outlined in this book would help with those relationships, but our earlier book *The Grief Recovery Handbook* might serve you better. You will find some duplication of what you've read and done in this

book, but it is more clearly aimed at those other relationships.

Here is an example of what we mean: John was
raised in a home with a violent alcoholic father. During
his many violent rages he used to hit John, always from
the neck up. As you might imagine, John learned to
protect his head very early in life. Not only did he learn
to protect his head but he had ample opportunities to
practice this skill. He practiced so much that protection
of his head became a habit. Eventually he used that
habit without conscious thought.

Years later, John's father died. Pay close attention to
the rest of the story.

*In 1979, it became clear to me that I was emotionally
incomplete in my relationship with my father. So, practicing
what I teach led me to do a relationship graph and a completion letter. I felt a great sense of relief as the result. Just as
shown in this book, I wrote a few PS letters as things came up
over time. For the most part, I felt totally finished with my
past relationship with my father. But I didn't feel and didn't
know that hidden below the surface of my conscious awareness was a habit that I was still using. I was still employing
it even though the reason for the habit no longer existed.*

*In 1983, my wife and I were at a party at a friend's
house. During the party a dear old friend of mine came to me
and asked if he could share an observation with me. "No
problem," I said. He went on to say that he had watched my
wife try to touch my head three times that evening and that
each time I hadn't let her do it. When he said that, I denied*

*it right away. He said, "You're very skilled at not letting her
do it." Then he asked the key question. "Have you ever experienced trauma to your head over a long period of time?"*

*When he finished his question, my mind zoomed back to
being eight years old. I saw myself protecting my head from
yet another attack from my father. With the help of a friend,
I had just discovered a piece of baggage that I had been
unconsciously carrying around for many years. I was still protecting my head from attack by a man who'd been dead for
seventeen years. I had discovered an old habit that would need
to be changed.*

*That very night, with the help of my wife, I set about
changing that old habit. Within a very short time I had a new
habit. I regained my choice about letting my head be touched
or not.*

Now Our Completion with You

It wouldn't make sense for us to close this book without proper completion with you. Although we haven't
been able to see you and talk to you directly, we have a
sense of you because of the many people we've walked
through the same actions in this book. When we help
people we feel very connected to them for their
courage and honesty as well as who they are.

So we'll close with this: Thank you for trusting us
and taking the actions we've shown you. We love you.
Good-bye.

Russell and John

RESOURCES: ONGOING SUPPORT AND SERVICES UNDER THE GRIEF & RECOVERY BANNER

The Grief Recovery Institute® is dedicated to helping people deal with the grief caused by losses of all kinds. While grief is the normal and natural reaction to all losses, most people have lost the natural ability to recover from those losses. Reeducating and guiding people to recovery is the primary objective of all our programs.

The Grief Recovery Handbook is available on our website, www.grief.net, and at all major retail and online bookstores. If English is not your primary language, it has been translated into several foreign languages, Spanish, Swedish, Korean, Japanese, Hebrew, Farsi, and Lithuanian, so far, with more on the way.

If you have children, you might want to pick up a copy of our other book, *When Children Grieve*. It was written in response to the thousands of requests we received for better information for helping children who had experienced a loss of some kind. An entire section addresses the first romantic breakup that your son or daughter will eventually have. It is filled with valuable information to help them grieve and complete this first monumental romantic loss. You may be assured that it will not tell you to use the "plenty of fish in the sea" statement. This book is also widely available and in several languages. If money is an issue, check the books out at your local library.

Major Programs of the Grief Recovery Institute

The two-and-a-half-day Relationship Recovery Seminar is for anyone who is struggling with the aftermath of a breakup or an accumulation of failed romantic relationships. This weekend event has also proved to be very helpful for individuals having a hard time in a relationship.

The four-day Grief ❣ Recovery® Professional Certification Training program is for those who want to help people deal with loss. Experiential and didactic, this program trains professionals and others in the specific techniques of Grief ♥ Recovery®.

Graduates of the Professional Certification Training become Grief ♥ Recovery® Specialists and are authorized to use our registered heart logo ♥ to announce their connection to the Institute. Please look for it when seeking the help that is suggested in all our books—this one, *The Grief Recovery Handbook*, and *When Children Grieve*.

Grief ♥ Recovery® Specialists offer the following programs to assist people and their children in dealing with all the major losses that have affected their lives:

The Grief ♥ Recovery® Outreach Program is a twelve-week program facilitated by a certified Grief ♥ Recovery® Specialist. It uses *The Grief Recovery Handbook* as the basic text and has helped more than five hundred thousand people complete the pain caused by the death of a loved one and other losses.

Helping Children Deal with Loss is a six-week program designed to help parents and other guardians guide children in dealing with death, divorce, pet loss, moving, and other losses. It uses *When Children Grieve* as the basic text and is also facilitated by certified Grief ♥ Recovery® Specialists.

For information on any of our programs please visit our website, www.grief.net. You may contact us by e-mail at gri@grief.net or by mail or phone at one of our locations.

In the United States:
The Grief Recovery Institute
PO Box 56223
Sherman Oaks, CA 91403
888-773-2683
www.grief.net

In Canada:
The Grief Recovery Institute of Canada
RR #1
St. Williams, Ontario
N0E 1P0
519-586-8825
www.grief.net

In Sweden:
Svenska Institutet för Sorgbearbetning
Tegnérgatan 24
113 59 Stockholm
46-8-335040
www.sorg.se